TEACH Your Children How to Behave

Brittany Ann

EquippingGodlyWomen.com

Copyright and Disclaimers

To my amazing husband and our three adorably energetic children—none of this would have been possible without you.

Table of Contents

Introduction

It was 8:00 at night, and my husband and I were sitting in bed eating chocolate cake. It was our first day home from the hospital, and we'd kept our adorable little baby boy alive for a whole day—all by ourselves! We were kind of celebrating... but mostly just tired. Taking care of a baby is hard work, even when you're only one day in.

At the hospital, they'd given us very specific instructions so we would know just what to do. *"Hold him just like this—make sure you support his head." "Feed him every few hours. It's okay if it feels like he's nursing round-the-clock. It will help your milk supply come in." "Never, ever shake a baby. If you get frustrated, that's okay. Just put him down in a safe place and step out of the room for a minute. It's okay to ask for help."*

And we'd followed the directions to a T; nursing every few hours, changing his diaper as needed, keeping his umbilical cord stump clean and dry...

Taking care of a baby really isn't so bad when you know what you're doing.

As time went on, however, the rules changed. Toddlers don't need the same things babies do, and kindergarteners need something different altogether. And this time there was no staff of nurses to show us what to do. We didn't get a trial period. We were just expected to *know* things.

• *What to do when your toddler throws a tantrum in the middle of the cereal aisle because he NEEDS Captain Crunch and Mommy said no.*

• *What to do when your four-year-old keeps getting in trouble at preschool for pushing.*

• *What to do when your six-year-old has a serious attitude—and you're pretty sure you know exactly where he got it from.*

- *The whining, the "gimmes," the potty talk, the need for constant reminders... the list goes on and on.*

Do you ever deal with challenges like these in your home? If so, you aren't alone. Moms all over the world deal with these exact struggles every single day. They want their children to behave, but they don't exactly know how to make that happen.

After all, kids don't come with instruction manuals.

At the hospital, you may get some basic instructions and a copy of "What to Expect the First Year," but I have yet to hear of a hospital that hands out a comprehensive guide to getting your children to use their manners, play nicely with others, listen the first time, and generally be pleasant to be around for the next 18 years and beyond. That's all up to **you** to figure out.

So if you're like most moms, you do your best. You rely on your instinct. You try to remember what your parents did (or didn't do) growing up. You ask your friends and family for advice. You maybe read a book or two and try to sort through the conflicting information as best as you can.

But at the end of the day, you still feel like you're making it up as you go along. And you wonder if you're making the right choices or if you're messing your children up for life and you just don't know it yet.

It's a scary feeling—knowing that you might be failing your children without realizing it. No one wants to be **that** parent. Maybe you should start saving for therapy now. After all, therapy is expensive. Who can afford that?

Now, let's imagine for a second that you DID know what you were doing. That when your children started acting up *again*, you knew **exactly** what to do to get them to behave (without all the yelling or spanking). Or—better yet—that you knew exactly what to do to prevent your children from misbehaving in the first place. How awesome would that be?

You could actually enjoy spending time with your family instead of spending family time stressed out, trying to figure out how to deal with your kids' behavior—*again*. The same behavior you've told your children a million times to *please. stop. doing.* You could go places, have fun, make memories—it'd be great!

And that's exactly what I hope to help you accomplish with this book.

Now to be fair, let me just say up front that I don't have all the answers. The strategies that work best for my children may not be the strategies that work best for yours. And while my children are great kids, they certainly aren't angels. Plus, my oldest is only seven, so I don't have any experience raising teenagers yet *(that's a topic for a whole different book!)*.

But there is one big advantage that I do have—a degree in elementary and middle school education.

Because if anyone knows how to get kids to behave, it's teachers.

Think about it—a teacher's job *literally* depends on her ability to get 20-30 children to listen to her. Twenty to thirty children who may or may not have eaten breakfast, who may or may not have gotten any sleep last night, who may or may not have involved parents at home. Twenty to thirty children who may or may not have the supplies they need, who all learn in different ways, who are all at different ability levels and who really couldn't care less about whatever boring ol' lesson she's trying to teach anyway.

Of course, there's a whole lot more to teaching than simply getting the kids to behave, but if you can't get the kids to listen, you're toast. Might as well toss the lesson plans in the trash and say a silent prayer because you're in for a long, rough day.

And it's even worse if you teach in an inner-city school or you substitute teach (or both at the same time!)—which I have. It's fun. It's worthwhile. It's an adventure. But, man, is it exhausting!

So after spending years in the public school system, years in the local public library and years in my own living room, trying to figure out how to get kids to behave—I have a few insights to share. They work with my kids *(I have two very energetic boys, ages 7 and 3, and an adorable baby girl)*, and I bet they'll work with your kids too.

I'm calling it the TEACH Method, because that's exactly what it's designed to help you do—TEACH your children how to behave.

Yes, you can raise well-behaved children and enjoy your family once again. Let me show you how.

Bonus Materials

Excited to put the TEACH Method to work in your family? Be sure to visit http://equippinggodlywomen.com/teach-bonuses to find a variety of bonus materials and printable worksheets you can use to implement the strategies you learn in this book right in your own home!

- The +Positive Parenting Challenge: a 6-day challenge designed to help tired moms enjoy their kids more.
- Printable worksheets and behavior charts
- Special freebies for busy moms
- And more!

Visit http://equippinggodlywomen.com/teach-bonuses to get started!

Chapter One: Why Good Behavior Matters

Seventy-five percent of Americans think people are becoming ruder and less civilized, according to a 2015 study conducted by Rasmussen Reports. Yet, chances are you don't need a study to tell you that. From the behavior of the latest celebrities and politicians to the characters in your children's favorite Saturday morning cartoons, it seems as though rude behavior is just about everywhere you look these days.

And the worst part is—this poor behavior isn't just unpleasant to be around; it can make parenting your children more difficult as well. After all, it's not exactly easy to teach children about the importance of good behavior when so many people around them are not only behaving badly themselves but practically expecting your children to misbehave as well.

It's a strange occurrence I've seen time and time again—even from people who should know better!

- When I tell my children "No snacks. We're eating in 15 minutes," only to have family members completely ignore me and give them chips and cookies anyway.

- When my son knocks clothes off the rack at Target and I tell him to pick them back up, only for the lady working at the store to tell him *(repeatedly!)* not to bother because she'll just do it herself.

- When I try to teach my children not to interrupt, only to have friends stop mid-sentence to fawn over every little thing my children want to say.

Never before has teaching good behavior been so difficult—or so important.

So, with everyone around you allowing, and even encouraging, your children to misbehave, plus all of the normal tiredness and lack of motivation you feel anyway, is teaching your children to behave really worth the fight? It is. And here are five reasons why.

1. Your Children's Behavior Reflects Their Heart

*"No good tree bears bad fruit, nor does a bad tree bear good fruit. Each tree is recognized by its own fruit. People do not pick figs from thornbushes, or grapes from briers. A good man brings good things out of the good stored up in his heart, and an evil man brings evil things out of the evil stored up in his heart. **For the mouth speaks what the heart is full of.**"* — Luke 6:43-45

Think your children's misbehaviors are just a "normal kid thing?" Well, they probably are. But they're so much more than that.

Your children's behavior isn't just the actions they repeat. It's an outpouring of the condition of their hearts.

If your children have hearts that are selfish and greedy, they will behave in a way that is selfish and greedy. If your children have hearts that are stubborn and uncaring, they will behave in a way that is stubborn and uncaring.

So how do you get your children to be less selfish, greedy, stubborn or uncaring? You don't allow them to behave that way.

Your children's attitudes don't just affect their actions. Their actions affect their attitudes as well. Therefore, if you want your children to be truly polite, caring and well-mannered individuals who are a joy to be around, you need to teach them to behave that way. Get the actions in place and the attitudes will follow.

2. Your Children's Behavior Shapes Their Childhood

Every parent wants their children to have a great childhood. And yet, taking your children fun places, buying them newer and nicer toys, loading them up with sugary treats, and giving them all of the things you had (or never had) growing up isn't the way to make this happen.

Sure, these things are fun on occasion—we go places and have treats all the time. But they really don't contribute to a happy childhood as much as many parents think.

Want your children to have a great childhood? Set boundaries and teach them to behave. Sure, it isn't glamorous, but your children's behavior sets the foundation for every other thing they will do throughout their entire childhood.

When you TEACH your children how to behave, you set them up for success in school, in sports and in extra-curricular activities. You make it easier for them to make friends and get along well with others. You help them succeed and have fun doing it!

Whether your children need to take turns playing kickball, work together on a group project, stay out of trouble at school or simply invite friends over to play, good behavior helps make this not only possible, but enjoyable.

3. Your Children's Behavior Has a Huge Impact on Your Family Life

Of course, your children's behavior doesn't just affect their lives, it affects your entire family as well—as any parent with out-of-control children can attest.

When your children misbehave, your whole family dynamic changes. You find yourself spending more time disciplining than making positive memories together. You can't go to as many fun places or do as many fun things because you can't bear to deal with their behavior the whole time. You find yourself zoning out and finding other things to do rather than spending quality time with them. This, of course, just turns into a vicious cycle of more and more misbehavior.

When your children are well-behaved, however, everything changes. Your children are a joy to be around, so you find yourself actually **wanting** to spend more time with them. You want to go do fun things as a family, and you can. You can

actually make positive memories with them instead c
hand out consequences again and again.

Everything is easier when your kids are well-behaved—fo.
and your children.

4. Your Children's Future Career Depends on It

Want your children to get a good job someday? Then teach them to behave today. Not to be too dramatic here—but your children's entire future depends in large part on how well they learn to behave. It's true.

Sure, a two-year-old tantrum here or there certainly won't ruin much more than your day, but every time your children grow a little older, the consequences of their actions affect them that much more.

A child who cannot sit still in class may get poor grades, be mislabeled with a learning disability or fall in with the wrong crowd. A child who consistently has a poor attitude may miss out on fun learning opportunities that lead to an eventual dream career or fun church activities that have a dramatic impact on her faith.

And when it comes time to look for that first job, your children's behavior becomes more important than ever. Good bosses don't want to hire people who whine, lie, cop an attitude or can't be bothered to show common courtesy towards others. They want people who respect themselves and others, take initiative and do the right thing even when no one is looking.

The job hunt may still be a long ways off for your littlest ones, but the children you raise today will turn into young adults looking for a job before you know it. Better to teach them how to behave now, when they are still young and impressionable, rather than later when old habits are that much harder to break and so much more is at stake.

You Have a Responsibility

Whether or not your children's behavior bothers you, you have a responsibility as their parent to raise them to the best of your ability.

The church isn't going to do it. Your children's teachers aren't going to do it. Society isn't going to do it. That's your job, Momma.

In fact, the Bible makes this very clear. Raising great children is both the parent's right and responsibility. Consider these verses for example:

"These commandments that I give you today are to be on your hearts. Impress them on your children. Talk about them when you sit at home and when you walk along the road, when you lie down and when you get up." – Deuteronomy 6:6-7

"Do not withhold discipline from a child; if you punish them with the rod, they will not die. Punish them with the rod and save them from death." – Proverbs 23:13-14

"A rod and a reprimand impart wisdom, but a child left undisciplined disgraces its mother." – Proverbs 29:15

"Fathers, do not exasperate your children; instead, bring them up in the training and instruction of the Lord." – Ephesians 6:4

Hopefully you and your children are surrounded by a great network of people who love you, care for you and want what is best for you, but these people aren't going to do the hard work for you. They may even make it more difficult. If you want to raise truly great kids, it's up to you.

So—are you up for the challenge?

Chapter Recap

• *Teaching your children to behave is important because your children's behavior reflects their heart, shapes their childhood, affects your family and sets them up for future career success.*

• *Raising great children is your right and responsibility. You can't expect anyone else to do it—that's your job.*

Chapter Two: Are You Willing to Do What It Takes?

Of course, I probably don't have to convince you that teaching your children to behave is important. After all, you wouldn't have purchased this book if you didn't think it mattered.

The problem isn't that you don't know raising well-behaved children is important; the problem is that you don't always know HOW. You have a few ideas, but they aren't really working—at least, not as well as you would like.

But before we dive in to the "how," there are a few things you should keep in mind.

1. Raising Well-Behaved Children is Hard Work

Duh, right? Everyone knows that raising children isn't exactly a job for the faint of heart. It isn't easy. And yet, how often do we think it really should be?

Simply telling your kids to "Behave yourselves!" or doling out haphazard punishments here and there isn't enough. Not if you want to have great, well-behaved kids. And you definitely can't expect your children to automatically know what is expected of them without you taking the time to tell them.

No, you actually have to **teach** your children all of the ins and outs of good behavior. And that takes hard work. Years of it, in fact.

Every child is different, so you'll need to use trial and error to figure out what works for your kids. And as soon as you do, your children will grow up a little bit and require different strategies. And once you've taught one child how to behave, she'll have younger brothers or sisters with different personalities who will need completely different strategies.

You'll need to be consistent in handing out discipline—even when it's hard. Even when you're feeling tired, grouchy or lazy and when you'd really rather just lay on the couch and mindlessly scroll through Facebook on your phone. Even when you really want to go to an important event, but you have to miss out due to the kids' poor behavior.

You'll do your best, but probably still feel like a failure from time to time. Your kids will tell you you're "the meanest mom ever!" and you'll wonder where you went wrong. You may start fantasizing about boarding school or at least a solo vacation on the beach.

It's hard. It's tiring. But it's worth it.

2. Raising Well-Behaved Children Takes Time

Furthermore, even if you do manage to figure out exactly what you're doing and you implement the very best strategies for your children and your family, teaching your children to be well-behaved is still a process that is going to take some time.

After all, your children don't learn to tie their shoes in one sitting. Or write their names, learn Spanish or drive a car. Why should learning a large and complex list of situation-specific social rules be any different?

As adults, it's easy to forget just how complicated and vast the list of social rules we are expected to remember is. After all, most of us have had *at least* two to three **decades** to practice, our brains are much more advanced, and we're the ones who **make** the majority of the rules for our children to follow.

But our kids—they're just starting out. They're just learning. And they have a LOT to remember.

How are they supposed to know that if they throw a ball in the house, your vase will get broken? Or that if they swing their bat a little too close to their brother, he will get hurt?

As grown-ups, we know the risks because we've seen these things happen before. We can think into the future and predict what is likely to happen with reasonable accuracy. But children, especially little children, haven't made all of these connections yet. They're still learning. And that's going to take some time.

3. Raising Well-Behaved Children Will Require YOU to Change as Much as Them

Did you pick up this book hoping for some good tips and tricks to help your children finally behave? Well, you're in luck because those are what I specialize in and I have a ton of them for you coming up here in a minute. But, before you start worrying about how to get your children to behave, there's one person's behavior you're going to want to look at first—and that's yours.

While there is a chance that you recently adopted your children and their awful behavior was simply part of the deal, for most of you reading this book, the truth is that your behavior has likely had a significant impact on how your children have turned out so far.

While "bad" kids aren't always the result of "bad" parents and "good" kids aren't always the result of "good" parents, your actions as a parent do have a tremendous influence on your children and the choices that they make.

So, what kind of parent have you been so far?

Are you loving, involved and supportive? Do you spend plenty of one-on-one time with your children every day, doing things they like to do? How are *your* manners? Do you set a great example for your children, even when you think they aren't looking? Do you monitor their influences and set them up for success?

Or have you been too busy, too tired or simply too lazy to parent your children as well as you should?

Please understand, I am **not** seeking to pass judgment here. We ALL have room for improvement when it comes to parenting our children well. Even me. Even you. But we can never truly be effective as parents until we first take the time to fully acknowledge and admit the part we may have played in our current situation.

On the next page, you'll find a questionnaire to help you better assess your current situation and any attitudes or behaviors that may have led up to it. Take some time to really think through the questions and answer them as honestly as possible.

You may want to complete the questionnaire over a series of days so you can better notice the behaviors and patterns that are actually happening, not just what you can easily recall. You may even want to talk to a spouse, your children or a friend to get additional insights as well.

The more you can understand your current situation and any attitudes or behaviors that may have contributed to it, the easier it will be for you moving forward.

Chapter Recap

• *Teaching children to behave is hard work.*

• *Teaching children to behave takes time.*

• *Teaching your children to behave will likely require you to change as much as them.*

Chapter Three: What's Really Going On Here?

Below you will find a series of questions designed to help you take an honest look at your current situation and habits so you can find ways to make improvements as needed.

These questions are not intended to pass judgment on you, your children or your parenting. I do not know you or your situation, and some of these questions may or may not even apply to you. They are just to get you thinking.

Please be as honest, open and thorough as possible. No one else has to see this, and the more detailed you can be, the better.

Let's begin!

(Visit http://equippinggodlywomen.com/teach-bonuses to obtain a free printable copy!)

1. How would you describe your children's current behavior?

• It's pretty terrible. It's a never-ending battle and I'm tired of it.

• It's really hit or miss—it depends on the day or the situation.

• My kids are really great! Sure, they have their moments, but who doesn't?

2. How confident are you in your parenting abilities?

• I have no idea what I'm doing. I feel like a failure.

• Sometimes I think I know what I'm doing, but other times I have no idea.

• I know exactly what I'm doing (usually).

3. When your children get in trouble or misbehave, is it for the same behaviors again and again, or does it vary?

4. What behaviors or attitudes do your children need the most help with? (Or are you simply hoping to prevent problems down the road?)

5. If there are specific behaviors you are dealing with, when did these behaviors start? Are they relatively recent or have they been going on for a while now?

6. Have you or your children undergone any changes you can think of during this time period that may have led to the behavior issues?

7. Imagine it's five minutes before the kids typically wake up and you know they'll be up any minute now. How do you feel? Excited for another fun day with them? Or are you dreading the day before it even starts?

8. How often do you count the minutes until naptime, bedtime or until your children leave for school? Every day, occasionally, rarely or never?

9. What kind of example do you set for your children? How many of the following are you guilty of and how often?

❑ Yelling

❑ Hitting

❑ Failing to say please, thank you or excuse me

❑ Speaking in a rude, annoyed or sarcastic tone of voice

❑ Losing your patience

❑ Using your cell phone excessively or at the wrong times

❑ Arguing

❑ Gossiping

❑ Getting overly upset while driving (road rage)

❏ What else?

10. How often do you spend intentional one-on-one time with your children? Every day, occasionally, rarely or never? How long do you spend with them?

11. How much screen time do your children get per day or per week? What do they watch and/or play?

12. Would you consider yourself fairly strict or pretty laidback?

13. Have you set firm rules so your children always know what is expected of them?

14. Do your children know in advance what their consequences will be if they misbehave?

15. What type of consequence(s) do your children receive if they misbehave?

16. How consistent are you with following through on discipline? Do you keep your word every time or is it kind of hit or miss?

17. Do you and your spouse (or any other authority figures who watch your children often) mostly agree or disagree on how to raise and discipline your children?

18. Do your children have similar personalities or very different? Are they the same as, or very different from, you and your spouse?

19. Do you treat your children all the same or do you tailor their discipline to their age, personality and past behavior?

20. Besides yourself, which adults and children do your kids spend the most time around? What kind of influence do they provide?

If you find these questions difficult or discouraging—that's okay! The point of these questions isn't to point out your flaws, to make you feel bad or to dwell on your mistakes. It's to figure out what is really going on so we can fix it.

Every parent makes mistakes—it's a part of parenting! And the truth is, your children honestly won't remember the vast majority of them as they grow up. As long as you decide today that you're ready to raise the amazing kids you have been given—that's all that matters.

And hopefully these questions have given you a few things to think about as we move on.

Chapter Four: An Introduction to the TEACH Method

"I will instruct you and teach you in the way you should go; I will counsel you with my loving eye on you." — Psalm 32:8

Now that we have a better idea of how things are currently and how they might have gotten that way, let's turn our attention to the future. Whether you're struggling to discipline an out-of-control child or you simply want to set your young children up for success in the future, the TEACH Method can help you do just that.

TEACH is an acronym I've developed that will help you do exactly what it sounds like—teach your children how to behave.

TEACH stands for:

T – Tell. Tell your children exactly what you expect from them.

E – Example. Show your children exactly what you expect by using plenty of examples.

A – Assess. Assess, and help your children assess, the situation to look for ways to help them make the right choices.

C – Consequences. Present your children with a choice and follow through with the consequences.

H – Help. Help your children think through the situation and find ways to make better choices in the future.

The TEACH Method is based on years of research (both mine and others') as well as real life experience both in the field and at home. It's simple (though not always easy!) and offers several notable advantages.

Advantages of the TEACH Method

• **It requires no special training, materials or prep time.** You'll be ready to begin as soon as you finish this book—if not before!

• **It empowers your children to make good choices**. The TEACH Method isn't about punishing your children or forcing them to behave. It's about teaching and guiding your children to make the right choices themselves.

• **It's gentle, yet firm.** With the TEACH Method, there's rarely a need for yelling, spanking, shaming or any of those other parenting strategies that just make everyone feel yucky inside. You're lifting your children up, not tearing them down—without letting them walk all over you.

• **It can be custom-tailored to your family.** Are you naturally strict or more permissive? Do you tend to be more hands-on or hands-off? Either way, you can easily adapt this method to work for YOUR family.

• **It won't fall apart when you leave home.** There are no stickers, marbles or red cards to lug around. You don't have to teach Grandma a whole new system. Teach your children this method at home and they can use it anywhere. At school, at church, at a friend's house—anywhere! *(You'll just do most of the legwork yourself before and after.)*

• **It prepares children for real life.** As much as we'd all like our children to simply do as we say, asking for blind obedience doesn't really prepare children for real life. If your children simply learn to listen to you—what happens when they grow up and you're not around?

No, your children don't just need to learn to listen to you *(though they do need to do that too!)*; they also need to learn to make wise decisions all on their own.

With the TEACH Method, your children will gain the skills they need to make wise choices throughout early childhood, the teen years and beyond—even when you're not around.

Throughout the next few chapters, we'll cover the TEACH Method in detail so you can learn all about how it works. Then we'll look at several specific scenarios and special situations along with multiple ways you can handle each of them.

My hope is that by the time you are finished with this book, you'll have a whole new outlook on parenting and maybe even an entirely new family dynamic if you're desperately in need of one.

Parenting your children doesn't have to be a constant battle, and you shouldn't have to be on your children's case every other minute to get them to behave. When you TEACH your children how to behave, they begin to learn the skills they need to behave all on their own.

Let me show you how.

Chapter Recap

- *TEACH stands for tell, example, assess, consequences, help.*

- *The TEACH Method offers several benefits. It requires no special materials, it empowers children to behave, it's gentle, it's firm, it can be custom-tailored to your family, it won't fall apart when you leave home, and it prepares for your children for real life.*

Chapter Five: Set Reasonable Expectations

"If you love me, keep my commands." — John 14:15

Do your children know exactly what you expect of them? Do you? The truth is, you simply cannot TEACH your children how to behave until you first determine what good behavior looks like to you.

It's different for every parent. Some parents want their children to be on their best behavior at all times, while others are fine with letting kids be kids as long as it doesn't get out of control.

So, what do you expect of your children? What **can** you expect of your children? This chapter will help you determine exactly that.

Start with Your Goals

Imagine for a minute you woke up tomorrow and your children had magically turned into perfect, well-behaved, delightful children overnight. What would that look like? How would they behave? *(Since this is only in your imagination, feel free to dream big!)*

Would they play together nicely without fighting? Would they share their toys or clean up after themselves? Would they sit through church quietly or through a nice dinner out without throwing a fit?

Would they be pleasant and respectful? Would they speak kindly and use their best manners? Would they look for ways to help the family by doing chores or by helping take care of their younger brothers and sisters? What do you envision? These are your goals.

Understand What Children are (and are not) Capable of at Each Age

29

Of course, just because you want your children to behave a certain way doesn't mean that they are capable. Not yet, anyways. After all, fourteen-year-olds are capable of a lot more than seven-year-olds, who are capable of a lot more than two-year-olds.

So the question is: What type of behavior can you reasonably expect of your children at each age? While every child is different, here's what you can typically expect:

• *From birth to sometime until sometime around one year to 18 months:*

At this age, children don't really understand rules and discipline. You can (and should) tell them what you expect in very simple language, but most of your discipline will simply be redirection at this point. Misbehaviors at this age are typically the result of not knowing better.

• *From around 18 months until 3 years:*

At this age, your children can learn what behaviors make Mommy mad and what behaviors make Mommy happy. They don't yet understand others' points of view *(they may not yet fully understand that when they hit, it hurts the other person)*, but they can begin to remember that certain behaviors bring consequences. Work on laying the foundation, but keep in mind that, at this age, your children truly do not comprehend everything you're trying to teach them.

• *From 3 years to 7 years:*

From roughly ages three to seven, children begin to understand rules as a general framework for how the world works. Children are beginning to learn that certain behaviors are good and naughty, and that the choices they make have an effect on other people.

At this age, children understand that there are rules, but they don't fully comprehend all of the logic behind the rules and when they do and do not apply. This is why it's so important to be consistent at this age. Consistency helps the world feel orderly and predictable, which helps kids feel safe and secure within their limits.

• *From 7 years to 11 years:*

At this age, children are beginning to understand rules on a more complex level. They understand that adults are needed to set and enforce rules, but they have also figured out that there are multiple viewpoints, that rules may vary based on context and that adults aren't always right. At this age, it's common for kids to push limits and test boundaries.

On the bright side, it's also the age that children begin to internalize family values and make their faith their own—so that's good news!

• *Preteens and Teens:*

While preteens and teens may seem almost like younger adults some days, the truth is they are still developing cognitively. Teens increasingly base their sense of right and wrong on abstract morality, rather than what feels good or makes someone happy, but they still fail to adequately consider long-term consequences or all of the sides to each issue.

Compare Notes with Others

Another way to get a better sense of what's "normal" and not is to talk to other moms who have, or who have had, kids the same age as yours. Talk to friends and family. Talk to your children's teachers, pediatrician, daycare providers and Sunday School teachers. Read books, magazines and blog articles. What are other children generally capable of doing at each age?

Babycenter.com is one website that has a ton of detailed information about early childhood development. You can also sign up to receive regular "What your child should be up to at this age" emails, which I get and love for my youngest two.

Cafemom.com is another website that can be incredibly helpful as well. They have tons of groups for moms of all ages and personality types. While the advice can be hit or miss at times (you're bound to find different parenting styles), you can very often find some great advice, or at least the reassurance that what you're going through is normal and you are not alone.

Tailor Expectations to Your Children

Of course, all of the advice in the world won't help you if it's not what's right for your children. So what do your children need? What type of expectations can you hold them to?

Do your children have special needs, exceptionally busy schedules, major life transitions, complicated family situations or a lifetime of bad habits to overcome? Then you may need to adjust your expectations down a little bit—at least for now.

Alternately, are your children fairly quick learners, eager to please or clearly capable of better behavior if only you'd hold them accountable? Do you have an important event coming up that they HAVE to behave at, or is it a period of natural transition in which you can switch up the rules more easily? If so, you may be able to adjust your expectations up a little bit.

Set Reasonable Expectations

Now that you've done your research, it's time to decide what you can reasonably expect from each of your children.

Take a minute to list all of the different times your children will need to learn how to behave. For example, at home, at church, at school, at bedtime, at a restaurant and at the park.

Go through one by one and determine two things: What would your children's goal behavior look like, and what could you reasonably expect starting today?

Once you've set these two benchmarks, you'll teach the first, but accept the second.

For example: When heading in the restaurant, you might say "In a restaurant, it's important to sit quietly so that everyone else can enjoy their dinner. You may play with these toy cars as long as you stay in your seat. If you aren't able to sit in your seat, we'll have to wait outside until our food is ready."

Your goal behavior is that your children would sit quietly in their seats. Eventually, you'd like them to be able to do this without food or toys to keep them busy. Your expectation for today, however, is that your children will need cars to keep them occupied. You're teaching the importance of the goal behavior, while still keeping your expectations reasonable.

Be Willing to Adjust as Needed

Are the old strategies you used to use no longer working? Don't be afraid to make adjustments as needed. While it is important to be consistent, all the consistency in the world won't help you if you aren't being consistent with the right strategies.

Different ages call for different strategies, and just because something worked once does not guarantee that it will work forever. Plus, you'll naturally raise your expectations over time as you teach your children how to behave.

There will also be plenty of situations in which you'll want to make temporary exceptions. You may let your children get away with a little more if it's a special occasion or if they are so excited they can barely contain themselves. You may choose not to discipline when you know your children's misbehavior is the result of hunger or tiredness. Your rules are there to help your children. If they aren't working—change them!

Examine Your Motivation

As you're setting your expectations for your children, there's one very important question you will want to keep in mind: "Is this in my children's best interest, or am I just trying to do what's easiest for me?"

While raising well-behaved children will make life much easier for you in the long run, the ease of your life should not be your primary motivation. In fact, there will be plenty of times when teaching your children to behave will actually make your life more difficult.

You may have to leave dinner or the grocery store early in order to teach your children that actions have consequences. You may have to throw away a toy you JUST spent good money on because your children aren't taking good care of it.

The point of setting expectations isn't to make life easier on you; it's to help your children learn to behave appropriately.

The point of setting expectations is not to say "Don't bother me," but to say "You are capable. You can do this. I believe in you." and then to hold your children to it.

Chapter Recap

• *Your children may not be capable of behaving perfectly right now. Set reasonable expectations and work your way up to your goals.*

• *Base your expectations on what children are typically capable of doing at each age, but tailor your expectations to your specific children and family situation.*

• *Be willing to make adjustments as needed. Being consistent is important, but being effective is even more important.*

Chapter Six: (T – Tell) Tell Your Children What You Expect

"Pray that the Lord your God will tell us where we should go and what we should do." — Jeremiah 42:3

Of all of the classes I took during college, there's one education class that really stands out. The teacher, wanting to teach us how to give good instructions, asked us to write out the steps for making a peanut butter and jelly sandwich.

Simple, right? You put some peanut butter and some jelly on some bread, smoosh them together and voila! Sandwich. Couldn't be easier.

Until she told us to give her the instructions so she could make one.

"Take some peanut butter," we said.

She picked up the jar of peanut butter.

"Put the peanut butter on the bread."

She put the entire jar of peanut butter on the bread.

*"No, no, no. Open the peanut butter. Get out two pieces of bread. **Then** put the peanut butter on the bread."*

She stuck her hand in the peanut butter. After all, we hadn't told her to get out a knife.

It's like if you've ever seen the Mr. Noodle segment on Sesame Street. If there's a way to get things wrong, he'll find it.

And kids are the same way. Get 30 kids in a room and ask them to do something as simple as write their name on a piece of paper. Two of their names will be so small you can't read them, two will be so huge they cover the entire paper, one name be sideways, one name will be in crayon, five kids won't be paying attention and two kids will just look at you confused because they don't have a paper.

It's not that children are stupid or difficult. They're just doing what you told them—or rather didn't tell them—to do.

And as much as kids have a reputation for being self-centered, the truth is that adults can be just as guilty. We forget that not everyone knows the same things we do or we assume that other people will somehow automatically know what we mean.

But for children who are just learning—they simply don't know. They can't read minds, and they often don't have enough previous life experience to know exactly what we expect. They're just making semi-educated guesses and hoping for the best.

Therefore, the first step in empowering our children to meet our expectations is to tell them what those expectations are. Here's how.

Give Directions in Advance

Have you ever had someone mad at you for something you didn't even know you were supposed to do? Chances are your children have felt like that from time to time.

Your children aren't mind readers. They don't automatically know what you expect of them. Therefore, if you want them to behave a certain way, you need to explicitly tell them so—and in advance.

Don't wait until your children are already misbehaving to correct them. Give them their instructions ahead of time and stop the misbehavior before it starts.

Now, "instructions" might seem like a funny word choice, but the fact is, that's exactly what you're doing. You're instructing—or teaching—your children how to behave.

I do this all the time when I take my children places like the grocery store, church or the zoo. Before we even get out of the car, we'll go over exactly what type of behavior I expect from them while we're at our destination.

"Do we run?"

"No."

"Do we shout?"

"No."

"Do we say 'I want, I want!!'"

"No, that would be naughty."

"That's right."

The specific language you use will vary depending on the age of your children and how familiar they are with your expectations. After all, there's no reason to go over your expectations long after your children have already fully learned them. But until that point, it is absolutely worth your time to take 30 seconds to review your expectations ahead of time so you don't have to spend 30 minutes trying to get them to behave once you're inside.

Be Specific

As you give your children their instructions, it is important to be as specific and detailed as possible without giving so much detail that you overwhelm your children to the point of forgetting everything you've said.

Say, for example, you tell your child *"Go to time-out!"*

Where should he go to time-out? For how long? What should he do while he's there? You haven't told him.

If I were to tell my boys *"Go to time-out"* and leave it at that, one of them would come out after three seconds, while the other would sit there all day. One would take a time-out wherever he felt like it and probably switch locations half-way through, while the other would sit on the rug for about 30 seconds before scooting the rug so he could watch TV. Both of them have been known to bring a toy with them to time-out or to spend the entire time asking *"Can I come out yet? How about now?"*

And while that may sound naughty, the truth is, in every one of these situations, my children are still doing exactly what I told them to do. I told them to go to time-out and they did. They listened to what I said. It's not their fault they didn't know exactly what I meant. I never told them.

What I should have said instead? *"That was a poor choice. Now you will sit on the rug for a time-out. No toys, no getting up, no talking. I will set the timer for three minutes. When it beeps, come talk to me."*

Yes, that's a lot of words. But it's a lot less than *"Go to time-out. Where are you going? Sit over there. Get your butt back over there! What are you doing? No toys! Stop talking! I said, stop talking! I didn't say you could come out. Now you can sit here even longer... etc etc"* every time.

And again, once your children know the drill, you don't have to continue to repeat instructions they already know. There will come a point when you can say "Go to time-out" and leave it at that. But until you can trust them to know and follow your instructions exactly, it's worth the time it takes to go over them one more time.

Be Clear

Have you ever told your children "Behave yourself!" "Knock it off!" "Stop it!" or "You better be on your best behavior!"

(This isn't judgment. I say phrases like these all the time.)

What do they even mean? Do you know? Do your children?

That's like if I told you "Go run a company" or "Go build a machine." Chances are, you don't know how to do those things right off the top of your head. Sure, you may have an idea of a few things that would be required of you, but beyond that, you wouldn't really know what I expected or what you should do.

It's the same with your children. When you say things like "Behave yourself," your children don't automatically know what you want them to do. Sure they know a few things—like no hitting or shouting—but beyond that, they're pretty much just guessing where exactly the boundary lines are.

They can't hit, but can they tap, touch or hug? They can't shout, but can they talk in a normal voice or a whisper, or do they have to stay silent? If you say "Don't run away," how close do they have to stay? What if they walk instead of run?

Unless you tell them exactly what you expect, they're just guessing.

(This doesn't mean you can never say "behave yourself," of course. You just have to make sure you give the clear instructions first and save "behave yourself" as a reminder, once your children already know exactly what you expect.)

Alternately, be careful about using phrases that could be interpreted in more than one way. Take a phrase like "Do you hit other people?" for example. This one phrase could be interpreted three different ways: as asking your child if he *did* hit someone, if he *regularly* hits people or if he *should* hit people. To a small child who is still learning the ins and outs of the English language, it's really not clear.

Make sure your children fully understand what you're asking so they don't get in trouble for accidentally answering the wrong question.

Give an Explanation

When you were a child, did you ever swear you'd never use the phrase "Because I said so" when you grew up? Did you end up doing it anyways?

It's completely understandable. Kids ask a lot of questions! And sometimes, they aren't even looking for an answer. Sometimes they're just testing you, looking for a loophole or looking to argue.

In times like these, "Because I said so" is a perfectly valid response.

The rest of the time, however, you will want to give an explanation if you can.

Explaining the reason behind your decisions offers two main benefits:

1. It ensures you actually **have** a reason, and that you aren't just saying no for no good reason. *(Admit it—you've done it!)* Not that you can never do this; you just don't want to get into the habit of always saying no by default.

Why *can't* your children have pancakes for dinner? Why *can't* your children jump on the bed? Why *can't* your children have friends over? If you have legitimate reasons, that's great. But if not, why not loosen up and let them? These aren't the battles that are worth fighting over.

2. When your children understand the reason behind your rule, they have an easier time remembering it, following it and applying it to other situations.

Without knowing the "why" behind your long list of rules, your rules are just that—a long list of rules. And asking a child—whose reasoning and memory skills are still developing—to remember a list of 100 seemingly random, unrelated rules is a lot to ask.

When you teach your children the reasoning behind each rule, or at least a set of guidelines or a framework for making the right choices, however, those choices suddenly become much more clear.

So instead of telling your children, "No swinging bats in the house!" you could try "If we swing the bat in the house, things could get broken or someone could get hurt. Does that sound like a good idea? Or should we take the bat outside instead?"

And instead of telling your children, "Pick up your toys!" you could try "If you leave your toys all over the floor, someone could step on them. They might get hurt or your toys might get broken. Would you like your toys to get broken or should we pick them up real fast instead?"

Of course, if your children are difficult and choose the wrong choice, you're free to insist they do otherwise. As the parent, you have every right to flat out tell your children what to do. But if you believe your children are capable of making the right decisions themselves (and most kids honestly want to), why not let them?

Be Prepared to Give Lots of Reminders—At Least at First

You know how there are some waiters and waitresses who can take a huge order, not write any of it down, and still get everything right? Yeah, that's not me. I worked in the food industry for over a decade, and you better believe I wrote **everything** down. I still do!

I don't know about you, but if I can't remember something as simple as extra ketchup, it seems a little unfair to expect my children to remember every single rule every single time. *(But maybe I just have a bad memory? I don't know.)*

The truth is, your children are going to need reminders. Probably for a while. It's not that they don't want to behave— sometimes they simply forget the rules or get so distracted by everything else going on that they're just not thinking about them.

The good news is that there's a huge difference between willful disobedience and simply forgetting to take your dishes to the sink when you're done. If your children are generally pretty compliant, but just forgetful, just stick with it and it won't be long until their new behaviors simply become habit.

Chapter Recap

• *If you want your children to make the right choices, you have to explicitly tell them what those choices are in advance.*

• *Give specific instructions so your children know exactly what you expect.*

• *Give clear instructions and say what you mean so there are no misunderstandings.*

• *Give an explanation whenever possible to help your children better understand and remember the rules.*

• *Be prepared to give several reminders—at least at first.*

Chapter Seven: (E – Example) Lead by Example

"Go to your room!" my seven-year-old commands.

"You're not the parent!" my three-year-old yells back.

Why is it that no one seems to listen when I tell them to do something, and yet, five minutes later, they're repeating the *exact* same language right back to each other—and to me? Does that ever happen in your house?

The fact of the matter is—your children ARE watching you. It may not always seem like it, but they are.

From the time your children are babies, they're looking up to you for cues on how to understand and respond to the world. When they're scared by a loud noise, they look to you first to see your reaction. They see you eat a cookie, and they want to try a bite too. They see you walk, and before long they're toddling right along behind you.

It's incredibly common for little boys and girls to play games like house or doctor or to pretend to be whatever it is you do for a living. Whether you're a great mom or a not-so-great mom or somewhere in between—your children probably look up to you and want to be just like you in so many ways.

Most of the time, this is good. We don't have to specifically teach our children every single thing they need to know. They pick up on a lot of it all on their own. Traits like affection, silliness and confidence seem to come almost effortlessly.

Unfortunately, it isn't just our positive qualities our children pick up, however. They pick up the negative ones too. And these negative qualities can be some of the hardest to break.

Children Learn What they See

Have you ever seen the popular television series "The Big Bang Theory?" If so, you may be familiar with character Howard Wolowitz, an aerospace engineer who lives at home with his domineering mother.

As a viewer, we don't see Howard's mother—but we sure do hear her! Any time she talks to her son, she yells across the house. And when he talks to her, he yells rights back.

It's not difficult to figure out where he got it from.

And yet, how often do we create the same situations in our own homes and then wonder why our children are misbehaving?

If your children regularly get in trouble for yelling—do you yell?

If your children regularly get in trouble for hitting—do you spank?

If your children regularly get in trouble for having an attitude or speaking disrespectfully towards others—do you ever speak in the same tone?

I know for me personally, pretty much everything my oldest child regularly gets in trouble for can be traced right back to me. When I have a poor attitude, so does he. When I lose my patience, so does he. When I stubbornly insist on having things my own way, so does he.

Imitation may be the sincerest form of flattery, but there's nothing flattering about having a child with an attitude problem and knowing he got it from you.

Now, of course, there are plenty of things that adults can do that children can't do. You can give time-outs, take toys away, send your kids to bed early and all sorts of other things. But if your children are struggling with the same misbehaviors time and time again, and you see that they learned them from you, then perhaps it may be time to try a different approach—at least for a while.

The truth is we can't expect our children to be well-mannered and respectful when we consistently model the opposite for them. You can say "Be nice!" until you turn blue in the face, but until **you** are able to consistently live out the positive attitudes and choices you expect from your children, it's always going to be a battle.

What Type of Example Are You Setting?

Way back in chapter three, you completed a self-reflection survey. *(If you didn't do it then, go back and do it now.)* Once you're done—look for patterns.

Which of your children's behaviors have they learned from you? Or if not from you—from other identifiable influences in their lives such as grandparents, family friends, your spouse or television shows they are allowed to watch? Can you spot any obvious culprits?

If your actions and behaviors are teaching your children to misbehave and they're getting in trouble for it, that's not fair to them. They're only doing what you taught them to do, whether intentionally or otherwise.

Take some time to reflect:

• Do you always speak in a respectful, pleasant tone or are you often grouchy and irritable?

• Do you keep your cool when you get mad or do you run out of patience easily?

• When your children make a request, do you acknowledge them and react in a reasonable amount of time, or do you make them wait while you do something unimportant like watching TV or playing on your phone? *(Do **you** listen the first time?)*

• Do you badmouth politicians, celebrities, other drivers on the highway or your in-laws but expect your children to speak kindly about others?

• Do you go about your daily chores with a smile on your face or

45

do you complain about your family and their inability to pick up after themselves?

• Do you eat your vegetables and go to bed at a reasonable hour so you'll be ready for the day ahead or do you stay up way too late binge-watching Netflix, eating cookie dough ice cream and scrolling on Pinterest?

How can you reasonably expect your children to control their behavior if you can't control your own?

Or perhaps you're so busy running your family from activity to activity or you're so stressed out with work or your own personal problems that your children don't even see you enough to learn from your example.

Now, please understand, I'm not trying to pick on you or say that your children's behavior is all your fault. I'm sure you are a wonderful parent who truly loves your children and who is doing the best that you can.

And it's not just you. I'm also guilty of many of these things more often than I'd like to admit. I'm not perfect, you're not perfect, and thank God we don't have to be! He has enough grace for us all—parents and children included.

But if we're really committed to raising great children, then we have to be willing to be open and honest enough to acknowledge any part we may have played in the situation and dedicated and determined enough to do something about it.

It may not be pretty, but it's worth it.

Chapter Recap

• *Your children are watching and imitating you. It's important to set a good example.*

• *It's unfair to expect your children to control their behavior if you cannot control your own.*

• *Taking the time to identify how your own behavior has helped shape your children's behavior is crucial for moving forward.*

Chapter Eight: (E – Example, part 2) Teach With Examples

"In everything set them an example by doing what is good" —
Titus 2:7a

In chapter seven, we talked about setting a good example for our children. And while setting a good example ourselves is crucial, it isn't enough.

Setting an example is very passive. You can model good behavior day in and day out, and your children may never even notice. *(Or you may slip up once and teach your children a new bad habit!)*

That's why, if you want to teach your children how to behave, you need to get them involved as well. By leading your children through example situations and activities, you not only give them time to practice the behaviors you expect, but you have a chance to clear up any misunderstandings or questions they may have.

Plus, it's fun!

Practice in Advance

Say, for example, you want to teach your children to sit quietly during church. So you start with step one of the TEACH Method—Tell. Sunday morning before church, you give your children very clear, specific instructions about what you expect.

"At church, it is important to sit quietly so other people aren't distracted. They're there to pay attention to God, not you. That's why, when we're at church, we sit quietly without talking, with our hands in our laps and our feet on the floor. You can sing when it's time to sing, but otherwise you must be quiet until it's time to leave."

That's a great start! But just because your children cognitively understand what they are supposed to do does not mean they are physically capable of doing it yet. That's why they need to practice—to learn how to behave and to cultivate the new habit.

So you have your children practice sitting on the couch with their hands in their laps, their feet headed toward the floor and their mouths closed. The first week they may only be able to sustain this for a few minutes. After a few weeks of gentle practice, however, they'll be able to sit much longer.

Honestly, if your children can sit still for three hours on end watching Saturday morning cartoons, they can learn to sit still for one hour during church (and not all of that time is spent sitting still anyway).

Plus, this practice time is the perfect chance to see what misunderstandings or questions your children may have.

For example, *"What if I have to go to the bathroom?"* or *"Why can my little brother read a book quietly but I can't?"* These are fair questions, but the time to address them is at home, when you can have an honest discussion, not during church, when it's time to pay attention.

Practice Frequently

Just like with telling your children what you expect of them, having them practice their good behavior is also something that you must do more than once—likely several times.

This may seem like overkill to you, but it's not for a child who is still learning. After all, how many times did your children have to practice walking, speaking, writing their name or eating with silverware before they truly became proficient? Learning to behave is no different.

So practice every chance you get. At the doctor's office, in line at the grocery store, at home, in the car, at school, at church... All of these short, two-minute mini-lessons will add up over time. Stick with it and before you know it you'll have children who not only know exactly what you expect but who are also capable of achieving it and willing to do so.

Using Muscle Memory and Habits to Your Advantage

Have you ever heard of "muscle memory?" The basic idea is that your body has an easier time completing tasks that it has done before. Like riding a bike, tying your shoes or driving a car, the more times you do an activity, the easier it is to do and the more automatic it becomes.

Well, you can use the same principle to help your children behave. Sitting quietly, speaking politely and walking instead of running are all physical activities that your children are learning to do. And the more times your children do these actions, the easier the actions become until the point where they simply become habits.

Teaching your children to behave appropriately will likely be difficult at first. That's okay! It isn't easy to rewire the brain and change old habits. Hang in there. The more times your children practice the new behavior, the easier it will be.

Have Fun with It

Does the thought of having your children practice good behavior again and again sound terribly strict and boring? The good news is, it doesn't have to be! You can easily make learning good behavior into a game so that not only is it more fun for everyone, but the lessons are more likely to stick.

For example, you could:

• Have your children model how to behave and how NOT to behave. *(Your kids will have a ball being silly—as long as they don't get out of control. Then the game is over.)*

• Read or tell them a funny story about a person or animal and the trouble they got into. *(There are lots of great books at the library on this very subject.)*

• Pretend like you don't know how to behave and have your children remind you of the rules. *(Get really silly with this!)*

• Play a game like Simon Says *(it teaches listening carefully to directions)*, Red Light, Green Light *(it teaches listening immediately)* or Charades *(it teaches taking turns and self-control).*

• Pose an example situation and see how many different rules your children can come up with for good behavior. Silly rules count! *(For example: "How do we behave at the park?" "We don't poke other people's belly buttons. We don't get in alien spaceships. We don't do cartwheels down the slide...")*

• Cook, play a sport, or do a craft. *(These all encourage self-control, listening and following directions.)*

• Hold a competition to see who can sit quietly the longest. *(This game is the BEST for tired moms!)*

• Intermix silly questions with your instructions. *("Do we run around? Do we yell? Do we wiggle like a noodle? Do we say 'I want! I want?' Do we do the chicken dance?")*

The more opportunities you can find to practice good behavior, the sooner your children will pick up on it. Plus, it's a great opportunity for some serious silliness too. Your children won't even realize they're learning!

Chapter Recap

• *Your children may need lots of opportunities to practice their best behavior before they can be expected to demonstrate self-control consistently.*

• *If your children practice their good behavior enough, it will simply become habit (in most instances).*

• *Learning good behavior can be a lot of fun when you make it into a game.*

Chapter Nine: (A - Assess) Assess the Situation

"Let us examine our ways and test them, and let us return to the Lord." – Lamentations 3:40

Once you've told your children what you expect of them in a way that is polite, clear and specific, you've set a positive example, and you've given your children an opportunity to practice, it's time to let them loose to make good decisions or bad decisions as they will.

Letting them loose doesn't mean that you just sit back and let them do whatever they want, however. At least, not at first. No, you're still nearby, keeping an eye on the situation, and looking for valuable opportunities to TEACH your children how to behave.

Step three in the TEACH Method is to assess the situation, and help your children assess the situation, to look for ways to help them succeed. As the parent, you have two jobs in this step: to take preventative measures and to give a warning as needed. Your children only have one job *(but it's a big one!)*: to think before they act.

Take Preventative Measures

Benjamin Franklin may not have been thinking of parenting when he first coined the phrase "an ounce of prevention is worth a pound of cure," and yet the phrase couldn't be more true of parenting as well. The more preventative measures you can take before your children start misbehaving, the fewer disciplinary measures you'll need to take later.

This is especially true for the littlest ones. Trying to discipline a baby or toddler can be frustrating at best and next to impossible at worst. Children this young simply don't understand or remember all of the rules they need to know in an adult world. This is why prevention—usually through redirection—is so helpful at this age.

Even as your children grow, however, taking preventative measures can still make a world of difference.

For example:

• Make sure your children have been fed, are well-rested and have had a chance to run off any excess energy before you take them somewhere they have to be on their best behavior. After all, even grown-ups have a difficult time behaving appropriately when we're tired or hungry; it's only understandable that your children would too.

• Help your children find things to do to keep boredom at bay. This could be fun things or chores (or both). While some boredom is good, letting your children get too bored is just asking for trouble.

• Give older children jobs while shopping to keep them from taking off or running into things. Have younger children hold your hand, ride in the cart, or sit in a stroller while you shop. Personally, I have my three-year-old stand on the front of the cart while I drive silly (with sound effects!) to make him laugh. We also go very quickly and efficiently to keep the trip short.

• If you know your children struggle to sit still at a restaurant while waiting for their food, you could bring a coloring book, order an appetizer or play I-spy. We did I-spy at the doctor's office the other day, and it worked very, very well. *(Be careful with letting them play on your phone, however. Otherwise, you may start a bad habit that will be very difficult to break!)*

• If your children are beginning to argue and it sounds like a fight could break out at any minute, go stand right next to them. They are less likely to misbehave when they know you're watching closely. *(Teachers use this trick—called proximity—ALL the time!)* Plus, when you're right there, you can give them the words they need to express their views and work out their problems politely.

Sure, taking preventative measures won't work in every situation. After all, it's pretty difficult to prevent a behavior you don't know is going to happen.

But when your children routinely get in trouble for the same things or when you can see in their eyes that they are about to make a poor choice, distracting or redirecting them before they have a chance to can save everyone a ton of grief.

At the time of this writing, it's the beginning of summer break and we have been BUSY. Between trips to the zoo, the lake, the kids' museum, the gym, the library, the baseball field, the park and anywhere else we can think of, we've been going non-stop!

While I don't recommend this for every family, it's working really well for us right now. My boys have a TON of energy, and without a good way to release that energy, it wouldn't be long before they'd be picking on each other or tearing our house apart board by board. (Or so it seems, some days!)

By keeping them busy and occupied, I am helping them use up their excess energy and preventing a lot of misbehavior. We're also having a really fun summer.

Does this mean that parents must constantly entertain their children in order to get them to behave? Not at all! My boys have periods of downtime every day when they play quietly while I clean, work, take care of the baby and do whatever else I need to do. But just like puppies, some children naturally need more activity than others. This is what works for our family— find what works for yours!

Give a Warning

You probably already know to give your children a warning when they misbehave. That's pretty common practice, and most of us do it without even thinking about it, if only because we don't want to actually have to get up and do something about our children's misbehaviors.

With the TEACH Method, you still give warnings, but there's a different way to give them that's more effective—a way that empowers your children to make the right choices instead of simply threatening them before following through.

Instead of demanding your way, present your children with their options and then let THEM decide which option is best.

(Wait—hear me out on this.)

While letting your children choose may sound like a recipe for disaster, you may be surprised. Most kids **want** to do the right thing. They **want** to make good choices and make you happy. They simply forget, don't know how or get so distracted that they lose focus and perspective.

By asking your children to stop and consciously assess the situation, you not only send them the message that you believe they are capable of making good decisions, but you actually empower them to make the right decision for themselves.

For example, say your son is throwing rocks in the backyard. He's not thinking about the fact that the rocks are going a little too close to the house; he's just having fun throwing rocks. He's entertaining himself. That's good.

You could go out and yell at him. It would be effective. He would stop. But you'd also probably ruin his afternoon and yours.

Or you could go out and calmly say something like: "That's quite an arm you have there! But if you keep throwing rocks, you're going to accidentally throw one through a window and break it. Do you think you should keep throwing rocks next to the house or should you find a soft ball instead?"

If you keep your tone polite but firm, chances are that your child will make the right choice. You'll still get the desired behavior (your child to stop throwing rocks), but your child will feel proud and empowered, not ashamed, hurt or angry.

And if your child chooses not to listen? Well, then it's time to move on to consequences, but we'll get to that in just a couple more chapters.

Think Before You Act

The entire purpose of the TEACH Method is to get your children to think through their actions and make the right choices. Kids don't do this naturally, but they can be taught—especially with your help.

Giving a warning (as outlined above) is one great way to help your children do this. You're making your children aware of the situation, their choices and the possible consequences so they can make the best decision. Another great way to do this is by modeling the thinking process yourself.

As you go about your day, talk to your children about your choices and your reasons behind them. Be sure to ask your children for their input as well.

For example:

• *"We will go to the park in about half an hour. Mommy needs to do the dishes first so they are clean in time for dinner. If I don't wash the dishes, we won't be able to eat."*

• *"Daddy has to go to work so he can get money. Without money, we couldn't buy food or clothes or toys. After Daddy gets all his work done, then he'll come back home and play."*

• *"Grandma and Grandpa are coming over after dinner tonight. Let's get your homework done now so you don't have to do it later when they're here. Sound good?"*

Messages like these, as simple as they are, help teach your children important lessons about choices, responsibility, and actions and consequences. Make them a normal part of your daily life and eventually your children will begin to internalize this type of language as well.

Chapter Recap

• *Plan ahead to prevent misbehavior whenever possible. Distraction and redirection can work wonders, especially for young children.*

• *Use warnings as an opportunity to give children a chance to make a good choice, rather than simply yelling or giving empty threats.*

• *Model out loud what it sounds like to think through your own actions and consequences. Invite your children to offer their input as well.*

Chapter Ten: Your Children's Actions are Their Choice

"Hear, my son, your father's instruction, and forsake not your mother's teaching, for they are a graceful garland for your head and pendants for your neck." — Proverbs 1:8-9

You've set expectations and set a great example. You've planned, prepared, practiced, and prayed. You've redirected, given explanations and warned of consequences. You've taught, guided, challenged, loved and set your children up for success.

And yet, at the end of the day, your children's actions are ultimately their own.

Just as you can lead a horse to water but you can't make him drink, you can also lead your children along the right path, but you can't make them behave.

And it's at this point in the TEACH Method that you have to take a step back for a moment and let your children make the choices they will—whether good or bad.

As parents, it's easy to feel like failures when our children misbehave. After all, the way our children turn out is a reflection of our parenting skills, right? If we can't get them to behave, then surely it's our fault.

If only we'd spent more time with them... if only we weren't so grouchy all the time... if only we were more strict, more fun, more consistent... We pile on the guilt. Layer by layer. Until we can barely stand up under it.

But the truth of the matter is—our children aren't perfect. They are **going** to make mistakes, and so are we. That doesn't mean any of us are failures—it means we are all learning! And sometimes we learn the hard way. It happens to all of us.

Your kids will lie, throw toys, hit each other and backtalk. They will break things, lose things, destroy things and eat things. They may even sneak out, steal, wind up with the wrong crowd, wind up pregnant, or experiment with drugs and alcohol.

And I'm not just talking about the "bad" kids, either. Even the sweetest, smartest kids from the best Christian families can find themselves in some serious trouble. It happens all the time.

This doesn't mean you've failed. It means God's not through with them (or you) yet.

After all...

- *Moses was a murderer*

- *David was an adulterer*

- *Rahab was a prostitute*

- *Jonah ran away from God*

- *Peter denied Jesus and*

- *Paul persecuted Christians*

Not exactly a ragtag team worth bragging about! And yet God had important plans for each and every one of these people— plans that He continued to carry out despite their sinful choices.

Your children's actions are their choice, and sometimes they won't always make the right one. The alternatives will be too enticing and the benefits of behaving won't be persuasive enough.

Of course, you know this already. You deal with it yourself every day. Every time you cheat on your diet, fail to tithe at church, get into a petty argument with your spouse or read a trashy romance novel instead of the Word of God, you make a choice. And sometimes, the consequences simply aren't persuasive enough to get you to do the right thing.

As the parent, it's your job to educate your children about their choices and to help motivate and inspire them to choose the right ones. It's your job to teach, encourage, cheer and hand out consequences when necessary.

But sometimes, your best is all you can do. God isn't asking for perfection. He's only asking for your very best. So do your best. Give it your all. And then trust God with the rest.

And don't worry—He loves your children even more than you do. Even when they make mistakes. That's what grace is for. The children who drive you nuts today may very well still turn out to be amazing adults in just a few years. He's not through with you all yet.

Chapter Recap

• *You and your children will both make mistakes, and that's okay. God can bring your children through even the worst of mistakes.*

• *God doesn't expect perfection, but He does expect your very best.*

• *God loves your children even more than you do. They're in good hands.*

Chapter Eleven: (C – Consequences) Actions Have Consequences

"Do not be deceived: God cannot be mocked. A man reaps what he sows. " — Galatians 6:7

I still remember the day my dad threw my tape away. *(This was totally back in the day when we still listened to music on cassette tapes.)*

I don't remember what was on the tape—something upbeat— but I sure do remember how it made me feel. There had been no warning at all. I did something wrong. He threw my tape away.

I remember thinking, "If I had known that was going to be my punishment, I wouldn't have done [whatever naughty thing I did.]"

(I don't remember what it was. I do remember going and getting the tape out of the trash later...)

I don't know why that one particular punishment stuck out to me so much. It wasn't especially harsh and I really didn't care about the tape that much. My dad had probably given me several warnings (that hadn't registered), and I probably deserved it.

I just remember being surprised. Taken aback. I honestly wasn't expecting it at all.

I was upset because I felt like I had been given no choice in the matter, and I decided that when I had children, I would tell them in advance what kind of consequence they could expect.

Fast forward approximately two decades later, and while my parenting has definitely changed over the years, there's one thing that hasn't changed—my kids know *exactly* what kind of consequences they can expect if they don't obey.

Actions have Consequences

It's a phrase I've said to my children countless times: Actions have consequences. You can't just do whatever you want. For better or for worse—there's always a price to pay.

• *Touch a hot oven, you will get burned.*

• *Throw your toys across the room, they will break.*

• *Leave a sandwich under your bed, your room will start to smell.*

These consequences aren't the oven's fault, your toys' fault or the sandwich's fault. No one *made* you touch the oven, throw your toys or abandon your sandwich. Those actions were your choice. And when you choose your behavior, you also choose the consequences that go along with it—both good or bad.

Sure, in the real world your consequences aren't guaranteed. But in the safety of your own home as a child, knowing the consequences of your actions and being allowed to choose which consequences you will have is very empowering.

When you know in advance what the consequences of your actions will be, you can choose. You can choose to obey and receive the good consequences or you can choose to disobey and receive the negative consequences. It's completely up to you.

Empowering Children to Choose

Asking children to choose their actions and the resulting consequences is an essential part of the TEACH Method, and it's a strategy I use with my own children **all** of the time. Not only does it empower my children to make a choice for themselves, but it further emphasizes the fact that their behaviors are **their** choice.

No one is making them misbehave. I am not punishing them. **They** are the ones who decide exactly how they will behave and **they** are the ones who decide which consequence they will get. *(I tell them this all the time too.)*

How empowering!

*To clarify: I do not currently ask my children "What do you think the consequence should be?" though I absolutely would in the future as they get a little older. For now, I simply present them with two options—the good and the bad—and let them decide.

The If/Then Formula for Presenting Consequences

Whenever I present my children with their options, I generally use some variation of the same basic formula:

"If you [make a certain choice], then [this particular consequence will follow]. If you [make a different choice], then [this other consequence will follow]. What is your choice?"

For example:

• "If you get dressed quickly, we will have time to go to the library for a little bit before dinner. If you dilly dally, we won't have time to go. What is your choice?"

• "If you run in the store, then you will have to sit in the cart. If you show me that you know how to walk properly, then you may walk. What is your choice?"

• "If you whine, then I will know you are tired and need a nap. Do you need a nap? Or would you like to stay up and play?"

• "There is no running in this house. Would you like to go outside and run around or would you like to settle down and find something quiet to do? What do you think? It's up to you."

• "If you don't clean your room, I will do it for you, and I throw things away when I clean. Would you like to clean your room yourself or would you like me to do it? What is your choice?"

This format very clearly lays out your children's options and consequences so that they can make the right choices. Using this format doesn't set the actions and consequences; it simply makes your children aware of them so they have all the information they need to make the best choice.

When children choose between two actions, of course they will choose the one that looks best to them! Running through the house is way more fun than walking, shouting is way more fun than talking quietly, and nobody wants to clean their room (not even me).

But when your children's choices are reframed in terms of their consequences, suddenly the other choice looks way more appealing. Being allowed to continue playing is way more fun than having to sit alone in time-out, and going out for ice cream is way more fun than staying home and cleaning.

When reframed this way—in terms of consequences—the right choice is clear, and your children are far more likely to make it.

Guidelines for Effectiveness

Now, in order for this strategy to be effective, there are a few things you must do:

• **Tell them in advance.** It's best if you can lay out the actions and consequences BEFORE your children get upset, when they are still thinking clearly, though late is better than not at all.

I generally present the choices and consequences during step one (Tell), and then again as a warning in step three (Assess). This way, by the time my children have made a poor choice, they have had plenty of advance notice.

• **Use a neutral, pleasant tone of voice.** With the TEACH Method, you aren't punishing or threatening your children. You are respecting them as individuals by offering them choices and letting them decide.

• **Follow through on their choices.** If your children choose to take the consequences instead of to behave, that's their choice. No need to fuss and fight about it. You are simply giving them what they requested. Calmly tell them *"You chose to misbehave, so you chose to get a consequence. If you don't want consequences, next time make a better choice."*

• **Choosing is a privilege, not a right**. Your children should be allowed to choose as often as possible, but if they continually make poor choices *(or if they make a ridiculous choice like running in the road and getting smooshed like a pancake)*, then they don't get to pick anymore. When they demonstrate that they can be trusted to make better choices, then they will be able to pick again.

• **Don't hold a grudge.** No need for "you always" or "you never." Simply politely present your children with their options as though you were asking for the first time, hand out the appropriate consequences, and be done with it. No need to keep going on about it. *(Although if you're giving the same consequences time and time again without results, it's probably time for more effective consequences.)*

• **Don't just offer choices when they are in trouble—offer them whenever possible.** This will get your children in the habit of choosing. *(Where would you like to go today—the zoo or the library? What vegetable should we make for dinner—broccoli or peas?)*

• **If your consequences aren't very convincing, choose different ones.** We'll talk more about choosing the right consequences in the next chapter.

Chapter Recap

• *Actions have consequences.*

• *With the TEACH Method, you aren't punishing your children for misbehaving. You are teaching and empowering your children to choose for themselves.*

• *Your children's actions and consequences are their choice. You are not the bad guy or a failure when they make the wrong choice. It's their choice. You are simply teaching them and granting their requests for consequences.*

• *If your children consistently make poor choices, they lose the right to choose for themselves until they can be responsible enough to make better choices.*

Chapter Twelve: (C – Consequence, part 2) How to Choose Effective Consequences

"My son, do not despise the Lord's discipline, and do not resent his rebuke, because the Lord disciplines those he loves, as a father the son he delights in." — Proverbs 3:11-12

Now that you know how to hand out consequences effectively, it's time to start deciding what those consequences will be.

While there are several types of consequences you could potentially use with success, the TEACH Method relies mainly on natural and logical consequences. Not only are these types of consequences extremely effective, but they also provide a direct and obvious correlation between your children's actions and their consequences, which helps reinforce learning.

Read on to learn more about these consequences and how you can use them in your home.

Natural vs. Logical Consequences

Natural and logical consequences are very similar, but they have a few key differences.

Natural consequences are consequences that happen automatically without any outside intervention. There is a direct cause and effect relationship between your children's actions (the cause) and their consequences (the effect). You only need to stay out of the way.

Examples of natural consequences:

• If your child doesn't eat, he goes hungry.

• If your child throws her toys, they break.

• If your child drops a pair of sunglasses in the lake, they sink and are gone forever.

Natural consequences can be extremely effective, but they must meet two criteria:

1. The consequence must occur relatively quickly after the action.

2. The consequence must cause an appropriate amount of pain, discomfort or inconvenience.

You would never use natural consequences to teach your two-year-old not to run into the street or your twelve-year-old not to get a nose ring, but you could use them to teach your children to eat their dinner or to treat their toys properly, for example.

Logical consequences, on the other hand, are consequences that are directly related to the misbehavior. They make sense, but that do not happen automatically. You have to hand them out. Logical consequences are also commonly referred to as "the punishment fits the crime," and they must be respectful, related to the behavior, and realistic.

Examples of logical consequences:

• If your child spills his dinner, he is the one who has to clean it up.

• If your child hits another boy on the playground, you don't let them play together anymore. Your child can sit on the sidelines or you can take him home.

• If your child repeatedly slams her door, you remove it until further notice.

Often, the hardest part of using logical consequences is simply figuring out the appropriate consequence to give. With several options for each misbehavior, it can be difficult not only to think of a good consequence, but also to choose the right one.

Three common types of logical consequences include righting a wrong, removal from a situation, and loss of privileges or possessions. (The three examples above reflect these three types.)

Alternately, you can think to yourself: "My children are _____. This must mean they are/have _____. So they must need _____."

For example:

• My children are running through the house. This must mean they have a lot of energy. So they must need to go play outside for a while.

• My children are throwing toys even though they know better. This must mean they have forgotten how to use the toys. So they must need to put the toys up until they can remember how to use them properly.

• My children are giving me an attitude. This must mean they are so grouchy they have forgotten their good manners. So they must need to go lay down in their rooms until they calm down enough to behave appropriately. They can also apologize when they come out.

The beauty of logical consequences is that they aren't meant to punish, but to teach.

There have been plenty of times in my own family when I have handed out punishments such as time-outs or spankings and watched as my children simply endured their punishment, only to go right back to their misbehavior five minutes later. They didn't learn anything, and it was only a matter of time until they were right back at it.

With logical consequences, however, your children can see the direct correlation between their actions and their consequences (with your help of course!) so that they are better equipped to make good choices in the future.

Creative Consequences

Tired of handing out consequence after consequence? One little known and surprising benefit of logical consequences is that they can actually be fun! (Yes, seriously.) When you choose a "punishment to fit the crime," you can get very creative in exactly what you'd like that punishment to be.

(I wouldn't do this for serious infractions, but for minor misbehaviors—why not? As long as your children are still learning their lessons, who says behavior correction always has to be serious and miserable? Get creative!)

Examples of Creative Consequences:

• If your children leave their toys all over the house, send their toys to "Toy Jail." Your children can do chores to earn money to get them out.

• If your children kick others, they lose the privilege of using that foot. They must balance on only the other foot for 2 minutes.

• If your children are arguing or generally picking on each other, make them "hug it out" for five minutes. Every time they argue, increase the time.

• Make a "correction" can. Have all of your children write down a consequence on a piece of paper and add a few silly ones in too (Examples: skipping dessert, picking up sticks, doing the chicken dance...). When a child misbehaves, they have to choose one consequence out of the can—who knows what it could be! **Note: I would only do this with older children who are already well-versed in the TEACH Method, as it wouldn't help younger children understand the actions/consequences relationship very well.*

Speaking of creative consequences, just a few weeks ago, my seven-year-old decided he was the parent. As in, he was **literally** convinced that he and I were on equal footing and that he didn't have to listen to me.

This went on for a couple of weeks. It was awful. Nothing was working.

Until I finally decided, *"Fine. If you want to be the parent, you be the parent. But being the parent comes with a lot of responsibility. Parents don't play toys, watch cartoons or play outside. They do work and clean the house. Oh, and they don't get to eat or go pee either—at least, not until probably an hour or two later after everyone else has eaten, the kitchen is clean and the babies are down for a nap."*

You would have thought I had told him he could never play again with the massive temper tantrum he threw after that. But I stuck to my guns, and he spent the afternoon cleaning the house. And now, anytime he starts to tell his little brother what to do, all I have to say is *"Oh, are you being the parent today?"* and you better believe he changes his behavior *real* fast! He learned his lesson.

See, I told you consequences could be fun.

A Note on Consistency

At this point, you may be wondering "But isn't it important to be consistent? How can you be consistent when you're giving different consequences all of the time?"

That's a great question.

Yes, it is important to be consistent. But being consistent doesn't mean that you always give out the exact same consequences every time, regardless of the infraction. It means that you are consistent with your rules and your follow through. It means that if something is naughty today, it's naughty every day, and if you say you are going to give a certain consequence, you do.

For example, if you let your children run through the house sometimes and sometimes you do not, that's not being consistent. They won't know whether they are allowed to run or not, and so they will take their chances and see if they can get away with it.

Similarly, if your children are never allowed to run through the house but sometimes you hand out consequences and other times you are too tired or distracted to deal with it, that's not being consistent. And again, they won't know whether you will hand out consequences or not, and so they will take their chances and see if they can get away with it.

Alternately, if you tell your children "These are the rules; these are the consequences" and you follow through every single time with no more than one warning, that's being consistent, and your children will know that you are serious.

Anything less and you are simply teaching your children **not** to listen to you because you probably won't follow through. And nobody wants that.

Chapter Recap

• *Using natural and logical consequences helps children see the relationship between their actions and consequences.*

• *Natural consequences work when the consequences happen within a short period of time and are of an appropriate severity. If natural consequences aren't appropriate, use logical consequences—and don't be afraid to get creative!*

• *Being consistent doesn't mean you always give the same punishment for every misbehavior. Consistency means your rules are the same every day and you always follow through with no more than one warning.*

Chapter Thirteen: (H – Help) Help Your Children Process their Consequences

"You're the meanest mom in the whole world! You never want me to have any fun!"

It was only a matter of time, I suppose. He made it to six before he decided I was a mean mommy. Some moms hear "I hate you," so I imagine I got off pretty easy.

That doesn't mean it didn't hurt, though. Just a little.

After all, this was my firstborn son. The one I'd lovingly attended to every minute of every day for six whole years! *(Okay, most of the time. Let's be real here.)*

I'd nursed him and rocked him to sleep. I'd taught him to walk and bandaged his skinned knees. I'd held his hand on his first day of school and worried endlessly when he wasn't feeling well.

But in this minute, none of that mattered. Here I was, the mean mommy. The one who wouldn't let him do what he wanted to do.

The truth is, children don't automatically understand why you have the rules you do or why you give them consequences for the poor choices they make. All they know is that they want to do something fun, and you won't let them. You make them do things they don't want to do instead.

You make them eat their peas, share their toys and put on a jacket when it's cold. You make them take baths, brush their teeth and go to bed at a reasonable hour. You make them clean their rooms before they go out to play, and you don't let them have sleepovers on school nights.

You're a mean mommy.

And while part of growing up is learning to deal with

disappointment *(after all, we can't all have everything we want all of the time)*, that doesn't mean you have to make your children deal with it all on their own. You can help them understand and process the situation so the lesson they learn isn't "Mommy's mean," but "When I make good choices, good things happen, and when I make bad choices, bad things happen."

The more children understand, the more likely they are to make good choices and accept consequences with a positive attitude, and the easier the entire process is for everyone.

Sure, young toddlers may not understand much at first. But they can learn. And you can TEACH them.

The day my son told me I was a mean mommy, we had a conversation. It's a conversation we've had a few times since then and a conversation I'm sure we'll have again in the future.

It was a polite conversation. I wasn't yelling at him, shaming him or punishing him, and he wasn't in trouble. I was simply explaining to him how the world works—at least in this house.

And it went something like this:

"When you grow up, do you want to be a nice person who listens and is a good friend, or do you want to be a mean person who is rude and obnoxious?"

"Nice person."

"Good. Well, it's my job as your mother to teach you how to behave. I'm not raising you to grow up to be someone who is mean or who doesn't know how to control himself. I'm raising you to grow up to be a great person who makes good choices. And the way I do that is by telling you how to behave and by giving you consequences when you choose not to behave.

I know you don't like your consequences. That's the point. You aren't supposed to like them. But if you don't want consequences, then you need to make better choices. When you make a good choice, you get good consequences, and when you make a bad choice, you get bad consequences. It's up to you."

By this point, he's listening intently. It's starting to make sense.

"Today, you made a bad choice. So you got the bad consequence. What do you think you'll do next time? Will you learn your lesson and make a good choice so you can have a good consequence? Or will you make a bad choice again and get another bad consequence?"

"Good choice."

"Good, I thought so. Now, give me a hug."

And so we hug, he scampers off to play and we're fine. He's starting to understand that mommy isn't a big meanie who punishes him for no good reason. Mommy loves him, and that's why she teaches him right from wrong. And it's in **his** best interest to learn.

We do this on a smaller scale quite frequently as well.

When he misbehaves, I'll ask him *"What did you do that was wrong? Why was it wrong? What are you going to do next time?"*

With these three questions, he's practicing honesty and taking ownership of the situation, he's processing and attempting to understand the situation, and he's consciously visualizing what making a good choice looks like. Even if he isn't physically carrying out that choice right then, he's choosing it. He's practicing making the right choice.

And the more times we go through this process, the more he learns and the more his behavior improves. Because it really does stick when he understands what is happening and why. Sure, he's not perfect. He's a child. But he's learning.

Now, are there children out there who stubbornly and rebelliously choose the wrong actions? Absolutely. And sometimes there are other things going on or other needs that need to be met. I'm not a clinical psychologist, and purposeful, persistent misbehavior and behavior disorders are both outside of the scope of this book.

But for your average child who really is a good kid and wants to behave but who doesn't always make the right choices, the TEACH Method works.

Chapter Recap

• *Your children may not like you very much when you hand out consequences. That's okay.*

• *Your job as your children's parent is not to get your children to like you, but to help them grow up to be great, God-loving, responsible adults.*

• *By helping your children connect their actions to their consequences, you empower them to make better choices in the future.*

Chapter Fourteen: The TEACH Method from Start to Finish

Okay, that was a lot of information. Hopefully I've explained it in a way that makes sense, but just in case, let's see an example from start to finish.

Pretend for a minute that I am going to take my children to see the new kids' movie at the movie theater. In our hypothetical example, they've never been to the movie theater before, so I don't expect them to automatically know how to behave.

Here is how I would TEACH my children how to behave at the movies. *(See if you can identify all the parts of the TEACH Method. They aren't all necessarily in order...)*

Before We Leave the House:

Me: "So, guess what. Daddy and I are going to take you somewhere fun tonight! We're going to go to the movie theater and see the new kids' movie. Does that sound like fun?"

Children: "Yay! When are we going?"

Me: "After dinner. Before we go though, I want to talk about how we behave in a movie theater. When we get there it will be very dark, and there will be a lot of people. It's important that we stay in our seats and be quiet so we don't distract other people who are trying to watch the movie. We might even get some snacks if you eat a good dinner before we go."

Children: "Hooray!"

(Depending on where we are going, sometimes we'll hop on YouTube and watch videos of various places like a parade or the dentist's office, etc, so they have a better idea of what we're going to do at our destination. We wouldn't in this instance.)

On the Way:

Me: "Alright, we're almost there! Are you excited?"

Children: "Yeah! We're going to see a movie!"

Me: "Does everyone remember how we behave at the movie theater? Do we run around? [No] Do we talk and be noisy? [No] Do we throw popcorn? [No] Do we sit in our seats and watch the movie? [Yes] Can you show me how you behave at a movie theater?"

Both boys sit very still and quiet with their hands in their laps.

Me: "Good. Because if you boys get too rambunctious and distract other people, we'll have to leave the theater and not watch the movie, and that wouldn't be any fun. So we're going to be on our best behavior so we can stay and watch it. I bet it will be really funny!"

Inside the Theater:

By this point, the children would already know exactly how to behave (sit still and quiet) and exactly what the consequences would be for misbehaving (leave the theater), so I wouldn't need to say much of anything inside.

If they did start to get rambunctious a simple "Do we get out of our seats?" or "Oh, are you being noisy? Do we need to go out?" is generally enough of a warning to keep them on track. I might also buy the kids some popcorn to keep them occupied or move my three-year-old onto my lap so he isn't so distracted.

While my goals would be for my children to sit very still, stay quiet, eat popcorn without spilling any and enjoy the movie, I know that those expectations are a little much for my youngest. Therefore, I would tell the children what I expected, but not get upset if my youngest switched seats quickly before sitting back down, accidentally spilled popcorn or made a couple of cute exclamations throughout the movie.

Leaving the Theater:

Me: "You boys were so good in the theater! I am so proud of you! Did you like the movie? What was your favorite part? ... When you boys behave, we all have a great time and I know that I can bring you back again. Would you like to come again sometime?"

-OR-

Me: *(in a stern, serious voice, but not yelling)* "Wow, that was not the kind of behavior I expect in the movie theater. You weren't sitting in your seats/you were loud/you were kicking the chairs in front of us... When you behave that way, it distracts other people and they can't enjoy the movie. That's why we had to leave—so other people could watch the movie without little boys distracting them. Maybe next time you'll sit nicely so you can stay and watch the movie. This time, we're going home."

At this point, you may be tempted to listen to your children's whining and give them another chance and another and another... Don't. If you've already given them a warning, then they've already chosen their behavior and their consequences.

Every time you don't follow through with the predetermined consequences you're essentially teaching them "Actions **don't** have consequences—you can do whatever you want and get away with it," as well as "When I tell you to behave, it's completely optional. You can do whatever you want; I'm not going to do anything about it."

You're also teaching your children that whining works. And every time that whining works, you're that much more likely to hear it again in the future.

You set your expectations. You gave a warning. Your children made their decision. Now it's time to follow through.

And that's the TEACH Method in action!

Chapter Fifteen: Practical Strategies for Common Behavior Problems

"Whoever spares the rod hates their children, but the one who loves their children is careful to discipline them." — Proverbs 13:24

Now that you understand how the TEACH Method works—let's put it to work for you. In this chapter, we'll take a look at some of the most common problems parents face today along with a few ways we can deal with each of them.

Obviously, it would be impossible to cover every single behavior problem you could potentially deal with as a parent or every possible solution that could work, but these ideas should get you off to a good start.

Behavior problems are arranged alphabetically.

How to Deal With: Arguing (among siblings)

For kids who love each other, siblings sure can fight a lot! Here are a few strategies to help keep the peace.

• **Keep them busy.** While sibling fighting may seem like a huge deal, oftentimes the biggest problem is simply that the kids are bored. Give them something to do. Chances are there are toys that need picking up, dishes that need washing or flower beds that need weeding...

• **Separate them.** If your children can't play nicely together, then they don't need to play together at all. Have them choose separate toys, send them to separate rooms, or have one play inside while the other plays outside. Sometimes even the best of friends need a little time apart for a while (especially if they share a room).

• **Have them solve their own problems.** If your children are older and know how to behave, have the solve their own problems instead of constantly running to you to referee. Ask them to come with a solution that is fair to both of them, or simply set the timer for two minutes and say "You have two minutes to come up with a solution, or I will come up with a solution for you (and you probably won't like it very much)." Oftentimes that's just the motivation they need!

• **Solve their problems for them**. The first few times your children fight, you will want to teach them strategies to help them solve their problems in a peaceful way—strategies like taking turns, finding different toys to play with or playing together. If they're old enough to know better and they're still fighting, though, put an end to it once and for all.

Are your children fighting over a toy? Take the toy away. Problem solved. Are they fighting over who gets to go first? No one gets to go. Problem solved. Show your children that they aren't going to like your solutions and they'll be that much more motivated to come up with some good ones all on their own.

How to Deal With: Backtalk

If you can't ask your children to do something without getting an attitude or an argument, you may be dealing with backtalk. Backtalk is draining for everyone. Here are a few suggestions for dealing with it.

• **Foster your children's cooperation.** If it's always you vs. your children, find ways to work together instead. This may involve spending extra quality time together or simply rephrasing your requests so you are working **with** your children instead of constantly ordering them around. For example, you could try "We need to get this house cleaned up before your dad gets home. Why don't you get started on your room, while I get started on the dishes" instead of "Go clean your room."

• **Monitor outside influences.** Do your children have friends or family members encouraging them to backtalk? Do they watch television shows or listen to songs that encourage it? Do other adults let them get away with it? Make sure you're paying attention!

• **Don't engage in arguments.** Just because your children love to argue does not mean that you have to participate. This is the perfect time to say those lovely parenting phrases like "Because I said so," "What did I say?" or "I said no. No means no." And if they continue arguing, just start handing out consequences.

You are the parent. You make the rules. It's nice if you have cooperation, but at the end of the day, what you say goes. Be polite, but firm.

How to Deal With: Bedtime

While bedtime is many parents' favorite part of the day, going to bed isn't such a joyous occasion for little ones who want to stay up and play. Here are a few suggestions for making the process easier for everyone.

• **Make sure your children are tired but not too tired.** If your children aren't tired, they won't go to sleep, but if they are overtired, they'll be cranky and wired. Try to hit that sweet spot when they are starting to lose some steam but they haven't started yawning yet.

• **Maintain a consistent routine.** Keep the exact same routine night after night so your bedtime ritual becomes a familiar habit. Your children are less likely to fight routines they do every single day.

• **Give them something to look forward to.** Make snuggles or story time the last part of your bedtime routine instead of the first (or instead of skipping them altogether). Your children will be much more motivated to brush their teeth and put their pajamas on if they know you're waiting by their bed with a story as soon as they're done.

• **Make it fun!** Instead of ordering your children around and rushing as quickly as you can, find ways to make bedtime relaxing and fun. For example, you might race, fly, hop or slither to the bathroom to brush teeth or you might sing silly songs before lights out.

• **Stay strong.** Dealing with children who consistently cry or get out of bed is incredibly frustrating, and you may be tempted to just give in to get some peace. Don't. Every time you give in to the whining or let your children stay up just five minutes more, you're teaching them that whining and negotiating work.

Put your children in bed, turn the light off, and walk out of the room. If they try to come out, march them right back to bed without a word or any other type of positive reinforcement. Set consequences for repeated misbehavior and follow through.

How to Deal With: Constant Complaining

Happiness is a choice. If your children need a little help seeing the positive side of life, here are a few ways you can help them do just that.

• **Model a life of gratitude yourself.** Go out of your way to be positive and to point out the good in life. Do this out loud so others can hear. Invite them to notice and appreciate good things too.

• **Have your children list three things they are thankful for**. You could do this in a daily gratitude journal, over dinner, or at the end of the day. Do this together, so everyone can share, and do it regularly—daily works well, or even every time they complain!

• **Make your children the problem solvers.** If your children constantly complain, put them in charge of fixing the situation. If they complain that they don't like dinner, put them in charge of cooking tomorrow night. If they complain that everyone else has things they don't, let them work (in or out of the house) to earn the money for the things they want. Get creative.

How to Deal With: Difficulty Sharing/Taking Turns

The good news is that difficulty sharing is a common phase most children go through. The better news is that you can help your children move out of it faster using the TEACH Method. Here's how:

• **Set an example.** If your children always associate sharing with "Mom makes me give my toys away," of course they aren't going to like it! Start by sharing some of your things with them so that they learn that sharing can be a good thing. You may say something like, "I have some yummy cookies here. Would you like to **share** one with me?" You can share books, toys, food, chairs—all kinds of things!

• **Start small.** When your children are still learning to share, make it easy on them. Have them share items that don't belong to anyone or that aren't their favorites. Have them practice taking turns, and keep the turns very quick so they don't have to be patient for long.

• **Remove your children from the situation.** For children who are old enough to know better: if they can't play nicely with others, then they don't need to play with others at all. Have your children sit on the sidelines or take them home.

• **Take the toy away.** Alternately, if you are already home and you have two children fighting over a toy, simply take the toy away. If they can't play with it nicely, they don't need to play with it at all. Your children will quickly learn that it's better to share than to not have the toy at all.

• **Don't make your children share everything.** As wonderful as sharing is, that doesn't mean that your children should have to share everything all the time. Think about it – do you share your husband or let all the neighbors drive your car? It's okay for your children to have a special toy that's just theirs as well.

How to Deal With: Dilly Dallying

Dilly dallying may not be naughty, per se, but it is disrespectful to others who are waiting, not to mention downright annoying. Here's how to fix it.

• **Adjust your expectations.** While your children's tendency to be slow can be quite aggravating, some of it may simply be par for the course, especially if you have little ones.

Instead of always rush, rush, rushing your children on to the next activity, why not slow down and enjoy life at their pace for a while? Too often, as adults, we get into the habit of rushing when there is honestly no reason to. Slow down, relax and enjoy!

• **Set a timer.** I'm not sure why this works, but it absolutely does (at least in our house). Instead of telling your children "Get dressed" or "Clean your room," say "I'm setting the timer for three minutes. I expect you to be dressed by the time it goes off." Apparently racing against a ticking clock is very motivating.

• **Make it a competition.** I use this technique with my boys all the time—because it works! Whether it's *"Who is going to brush their teeth first?"* or *"Who is going to get in bed first?"* it absolutely sends their little feet running. You don't even have to have multiple children to do this either. I race my three-year-old to his bed at naptime every day! *(Per his request!)*

• **Forego fun activities**. Of course, not every activity needs to be fun and games. Sometimes your children just need to obey, and if they don't, they miss out. Perhaps they only have half an hour at the library or they are 30 minutes late to practice because they took too long getting ready. You might even leave without them so they don't get to go. Actions have consequences. *(Obviously leave young children with a trusted adult, not home alone.)*

How to Deal With: A Disrespectful Attitude

Respect isn't optional. Not according to 1 Peter 2:17 anyways, which commands believers to "show proper respect to everyone." So how do you respond when your children cop a disrespectful attitude? Here are a few ideas.

• **Watch your language/tone.** When someone cops an attitude with you, it's only natural to get defensive and give it right back. Make sure you aren't inadvertently starting your children's attitudes without meaning to.

• **Foster love**. If your children are in the habit of mistreating others, give them opportunities to treat others well. Have them write kind letters, give compliments and find ways to help others out. Make sure your children are getting the one-on-one time and attention they need from you as well.

• **Show some understanding**. No one *wants* to get into arguments all day long. If your children are very angry, disrespectful and argumentative, there's probably a reason. It doesn't hurt to take a minute to talk to them to see what may be going on. This is a good time to empathize, but also to teach important lessons like "We can't always have everything we want" and "It's okay to be mad. It's not okay to be disrespectful."

• **Stay calm and give consequences.** Of course, even if your children have a good reason for a bad attitude, that doesn't make it okay. Stay calm, give consequences, and remain firm in your decisions. It's okay if your children are mad at you. They'll get over it.

How to Deal With: Entitlement

Do your children think the world revolves around them? While this is normal for babies, it's not so cute as your children grow up. Here's how to give them a little perspective.

• **Give your children work to do**. In our family, we have a saying, "Everybody helps," and we use it all the time. When children are expected to pitch in, they learn that keeping a family running takes work, and if they want things, they can put the work in themselves. No one is sitting around waiting on them hand and foot.

• **Help your children appreciate all they have.** Take them to volunteer at a homeless shelter, a battered women and children's shelter or on a missions trip overseas, if you can. Take them shopping for items others desperately need. Your children may quickly realize they don't have it so bad after all.

• **Balance your family budget together**. If your older children don't understand why other people have nice things your family doesn't have, give them a crash course in home economics. Have them help you balance the budget and ask **them** to make the tough decisions. *"What should we buy? Groceries or name brand clothes? Electricity or another pair of shoes?"*

How to Deal With: The Gimmes

Children don't automatically understand that money doesn't grow on trees and that they don't need every single toy they see. Here's how to help them keep their wants under control.

• **Set guidelines for when your children can and cannot have new toys.** The general rule in our house is that I buy our children new toys on their birthdays and Christmas. If it's not right before their birthday or Christmas, they know not to ask for toys because I'm not buying any. I simply say "Oh, is it your birthday?" *(I do sometimes buy toys in between, but it's rare and **never** in response to whining.)*

• **Make your nos binding.** Simply say *"No"* with conviction. If they ask again, say, *"I said no. I do not change my mind. Do not ask again."* If they ask a third time, it's time for consequences.

• **Set limits and give them a choice.** Make a rule or guideline about the number of new things your children can have and let them do the choosing themselves. For example "Only one new toy a month," "Only four toys for your birthday," or "For every new toy we get, we have to throw an old toy away."

Instead of asking you for every little thing, your children can decide for themselves which option they'd like the most. They only need to tell you their final decision.

How to Deal With: Hitting

No parent wants to be THAT parent—the one with kids who hit. Here are a few tips to help keep it from happening.

• **Hold their hands together.** When my oldest was a toddler, I used to take both of his hands together in my hands and hold them for 2-3 minutes so he couldn't run off and play. He *hated* this. But if children can't use their hands properly, they don't need to use them at all.

• **Redirect them.** Little ones often hit because they simply don't know any better. Let your children know in no uncertain terms that hitting is naughty, and then help them find better ways to express themselves or better things to do instead.

• **Rethink spanking.** While I'm not anti-spanking, if your children are hitting others, it may be time to rethink spanking—at least for a while.

• **Remove them from the situation.** If your children can't play nicely with other children, they don't need to play with them at all. Take them home or to time-out by themselves.

How to Deal With: Interrupting

To small children, every little thought they have is super important. Teach them to value your thoughts and conversations just as much with these helpful tips.

• **Teach them how to interrupt appropriately.** Figuring out the exact right moment to jump into a conversation is tricky—even for adults! Use the TEACH Method to teach your children how you'd like them to signal to you that they'd like a turn. Should they stand and wait, quietly tap your arm, or say "Excuse me?"

• **Set a timer.** If your children aren't used to waiting patiently for their turn to talk, they may need some practice. Set a timer for three to five minutes and instruct them that you will be talking to Daddy during that time, but once it beeps, they may have a turn.

• **Ignore them.** Children as young as three can learn not to talk when others are talking. If you've already taught your children not to interrupt and they do anyways, simply ignore them. Otherwise, every time you stop what you're doing and pay attention to them, you are simply encouraging the behavior.

• **Give consequences.** If your children can't wait their turn to talk, they don't need a turn at all. They can hang out in their rooms by themselves for a while.

How to Deal With: Lying

One of the more difficult behavior problems to deal with—because you don't always know if your children are lying or not—lying is one behavior you want to nip in the bud as soon as possible. Here are a few tips for how you can do just that.

• **Set a good example**. When's the last time you lied about your children's age to get them into the zoo for free or did something and asked your children not to tell their father? If you expect your children to tell the truth despite the consequences, you need to be willing to do the same.

• **Make your expectations clear**. For young children who are still trying to understand right and wrong, "wrong" is simply whatever makes Mom angry. It's no surprise then that they'd give whatever answer they think will make you happy—they're trying to do the right thing and stay out of trouble! Make it clear that you expect the truth, and that you'll be more upset if your children lie.

• **Word your questions carefully.** When asking your children questions about their behavior, make sure your questions are clear. A question such as "Do you hit other people?" could be interpreted in a few different ways, and you don't want your children to misunderstand the question or answer the wrong question according to a technicality or loophole.

• **Prevent future lying**. If your children lie repeatedly, take some time to really figure out what is going on. Are they seeking attention? Wanting to avoid trouble? Give consequences for the current situation, and then work together to find a game plan to avoid the lying in the future.

How to Deal With: Messes

Whether you have one child or six, you have better things to do than walk around behind them all day cleaning up their messes. Here's how you can encourage tidier behavior.

• **Have your children clean up after themselves.** Even children as young as two or three can learn to clean up after themselves. They may not do a perfect job, but they're learning. And anything they do is less that you have to do—both now and in the future.

• **Hold off on fun activities.** Your children want to go to a friend's house or to the park? Sure they can—as soon as their room is clean! Responsibilities first, then fun. If your children clean up, they get to go. If they don't, they don't. Simple as that.

• **Use natural consequences.** For older children, this may be the perfect time for natural consequences. If they don't put their dirty clothes in the hamper, their clothes don't get washed. If they don't take their dishes to the sink, you can't serve dinner the next night (because nothing is clean).

• **Be the maid.** If your older children need a maid to pick up after them, be the maid. But maids get paid. Your children can forfeit part of their allowance or do extra chores around the house to pay you for any messes of theirs you had to clean up.

How to Deal With: Mistreating Toys

You spent good money on your children's toys. You don't want them to get lost or broken. Here's how to help your children treat them properly.

• **Make your expectations clear.** Your children can throw a ball—can they throw a car or an airplane? Outside only or inside too? Can they stand on their toys? Which ones? How rough, loud or rambunctious are they allowed to be? Where are the boundaries? Your children won't know unless you TEACH them.

• **Take them away.** If your children can't play with their toys properly, they don't need to play with them at all. Take the toys away temporarily for a first time offense. If your children habitually mistreat their toys, give them away to other children

92

who will treat them properly (Goodwill).

• **Make them pay.** Why should you have to spend all your hard-earned money on toys they are just going to break? Have your children work (either at a part-time job or just around the house) to earn the money to buy their own replacement toys. Alternately, you can fix their broken toys, but they'll be responsible for paying for parts and labor.

How to Deal With: Negotiating

When you tell your children no, does it always end up in an argument? It's normal for children to push the limits to find out where they are. Here are a few ways to make them abundantly clear and end the negotiating for good.

• **Be firm in your responses**. Avoid giving wishy-washy answers like "Maybe if you're good" or "I'll think about it." If the answer is no, say no. If your children protest, say, "I said no, and I do not change my mind." Once your children realize that no means no, they will have no reason to argue or negotiate.

• **Set guidelines and be consistent**. When you are inconsistent with what you will allow when, your children truly don't know what to expect and they will misbehave just to see if they can get away with it. Set some guidelines or rules and stick to them. Post them up in a conspicuous place is you need to.

One thing that worked well for us was creating a daily schedule that I taped on my children's door. Then, they knew exactly when TV time, snack time and bedtime were. There was no need for constant asking and negotiating; they could simply refer to the schedule. It was such a sanity saver!

• **Allow your children to make a case—once**. Alternately, as your children get older, you'll want to gradually want to shift from flat out telling them what to do to helping them make responsible choices for themselves. Allowing them to state their case (once) is a good way for your children to practice critical thinking and decision making skills without letting them have full control just yet.

If your children are insistent, tell them they have five minutes to try to convince you to see their side. Spend these five minutes truly listening and trying to see their point of view. But, at the five minute mark, all negotiating stops, you make your decision and they live with whatever you decide. End of discussion.

How to Deal With: Not Listening the First Time

The most common reason why children don't listen the first time is simply because they don't have to. Every time you give your children another warning or you fail to follow through with consequences, you teach them that you don't mean what you say. Here's how to change that.

• **Pair a request with a reward.** To be clear, I am NOT talking about bribing your children. But if you save your requests until right before you're about to do something fun anyways, chances are your children will get done their jobs done a lot quicker.

For example, *"Are you ready to go to the park? Okay! Just get your shoes on and we'll go!"* and *"Dinner's ready! Pick up 20 toys in your room real fast, and then we'll be ready to eat!"* are a lot more motivating than *"Put your shoes on!"* and *"Clean your room!"* since your children will be anticipating the reward.

• **Stop giving so many warnings.** While one warning is helpful, giving any more is simply teaching your children that they don't need to listen the first time. After you've set your expectations and given one warning, follow through.

• **Set up situations where you have more leverage.** Go out for ice cream or to the park in the evening, and leave children who don't get ready at home with Dad. Or, if you're already out, take the children who don't listen home while the others stay. It's amazing how quickly children learn when you can leverage activities they love and hand out real consequences they care

94

about.

How to Deal With: Picky Eating

Despite the fact that America is the land of plenty, many moms worry about their children getting enough to eat. The truth is, for most moms, this really doesn't need to be a worry or battle at all. Here's how to make sure it's not.

• **Don't overreact**. While bribing or forcing your children to finish their dinner may work in the short term, it only sets you up to fail in the long term. If your children aren't hungry, they aren't hungry. They'll eat when they are, and missing a meal or two in the meantime won't hurt them. They won't starve over one missed meal.

• **Cut out snacks.** Speaking of starving, the problem may simply be that your children really aren't that hungry. Try serving fewer snacks or cups of juice or serving dinner later. This will ensure they are nice and hungry come mealtime.

• **Prepare a mix of new and familiar foods.** If you're having trouble getting your children to try new things, try expanding their palates gradually. Cook old favorites in a new way, add new ingredients to favorite recipes, or serve new foods alongside family favorites. Make the transition gradual.

• **Let your kids help in the kitchen.** Cooking with kids can be a lot of fun, and kids are more likely to eat their creations when they've had a hand in making them. Even children as young as one or two can help pour a small cup of milk or sprinkle cheese over a salad.

How to Deal With: Poor Manners

No one wants to be around children who are rude and

obnoxious—even their own mothers! Use these tips to help your children learn their nice manners so you can enjoy their company again.

• **Give a simple reminder.** If your children say "Give me that cup!" simply say "May I have the cup, please?" and wait for them to repeat the good manners right back to you. Oftentimes, a simple, polite reminder is enough.

• **Make a fuss.** I often make a fuss when one of my children uses nice manners. They love the positive attention, and it isn't long until the other one is chiming in with his nice manners so he can have a little positive attention as well. It works, and it's much nicer than yelling.

• **Insist on good manners.** If your children refuse to use good manners, however, refuse to listen to their request. Just ignore them. If they want something, they can use the proper words to ask for it. After all, you don't get a cup when you say "blanket," and you don't get a snack when you say "gimme!"

• **Remove them from the situation.** If your children are choosing to be rude, you can choose not to listen to it. Send your children to their rooms until they remember how to behave properly around others.

How to Deal With: Potty Talk

Tired of the constant poop jokes? I don't blame you. Here are a few tips to regain your sanity.

• **Don't encourage it.** Potty talk may be hilarious when your children are one or two. It's not so funny when they are seven or eight. Be careful encouraging this type of language too much when your children are little. It just might stick.

• **Monitor their influences.** Do your children have friends who think potty talk is funny? Do they watch television shows or movies or play games that feature this kind of talk? It may be time to make some changes in what types of shows or movies your children are allowed to watch or what types of games they are allowed to play.

• **Send children to the bathroom.** If your children insist on using potty talk even though they are old enough to know better, send their potty mouths to the bathroom. They can say things all they like, but only in the bathroom where you don't have to hear it. Chances are it won't be so funny without an audience.

How to Deal With: Selfishness/Self-Centeredness

With very young children, a little selfishness and self-centeredness is normal and to be expected. You don't want it to last forever, though. Here's how to make sure it doesn't.

• **Give your children a chance to do nice things for others**. Most little children actually love doing nice things for others. Sometimes they just need the reminder. Encourage your children to notice what others are feeling and respond appropriately, through sharing, hugs and kisses, kind words, or giving up a turn.

• **Be a little selfish yourself**. If you're used to constantly putting the children first or going without so they can have more, more, more, it's time to stop. This type of behavior isn't loving; it just encourages selfishness.

Make your children wait and share. For example, you may say "I will play cars with you—after I feed the baby" or "There is only one cookie left. You can't have it all, but I will share it with you."

How to Deal With: Sore Losers

In a world of participation trophies where everyone wins all the time, learning to lose gracefully can be tough. Here are a few strategies you can try at home.

• **Practice winning and losing**. If your children aren't very good at losing, that's okay. They just need practice. Play board games together and host competitions. Make sure your children win some and lose some, and calmly explain that that's the way it works. Sometimes you win, and sometimes you lose, but you never throw a fit.

• **Emphasize effort as well as performance**. Even if your children don't win, if they give great effort, that's still commendable. Performance does matter, but if your children truly gave it their all, acknowledge that too!

How to Deal With: Temper Tantrums

Big emotions can present a big challenge for little children who don't yet know how to deal with them properly. Here are a few tips to help little ones cope.

• **Prevent meltdowns when you can.** Children are most likely to have temper tantrums when they are hungry, tired or overwhelmed. Time errands to avoid the grouchy hours, if you can.

• **Help your children ask politely.** Sometimes little children have temper tantrums when they can't communicate their needs effectively and they become overly frustrated. Help prevent this frustration by giving your children the words they need to express themselves when they are upset.

• **Ignore it.** Are your children throwing a temper tantrum on the floor? Ignore them, step right over them, walk away and continue on with your day. You can even do this in a store, provided you don't wander too far away *(barely out of sight is* *perfect)*. Teach your children that temper tantrums don't work.

• **Send your children to have a temper tantrum somewhere else.** Say "No means no. If you'd like to continue to scream and kick, you may, but you'll have to do it alone in your room where I don't have to listen to it." Temper tantrums are a lot less fun without an audience.

How to Deal With: Whining

Children whine because it works. They know if they pester you enough times, you'll eventually give up and give in. If you want the whining to end—make sure it doesn't work.

• **Remind your children of the proper way to ask.** Sometimes with little kids, they want to use their manners, but they simply forget. A simple "Where are your manners?" or "May I have a drink, *please*?" (if they are demanding a cup right now) should remind them what to say.

• **Ignore the whining.** If the whining has become habitual, ignore it. Say "I'm sorry; I don't speak Whinese," then go about your day like you don't hear it at all.

• **Send your children to whine somewhere else.** Your children can whine all they want, but that doesn't mean you have to listen to it. Say "No means no. You may continue to whine if you'd like, but you have to do it in your room."

• **Give the opposite consequence.** If your children are whining for a cookie, for example, say "I already said no. Continue whining and you won't get a cookie tomorrow either." *(Be careful as consequences can stack up real fast.)*

Of course, these are just a few suggestions for actions you can take. Feel free to get creative and come up with your own logical consequences if you can think of some good ones! Find what works for you.

Chapter Sixteen: Troubleshooting and Special Circumstances

Not sure if the TEACH Method will work for you? Or have you already started implementing it but you're running into some complications?

While the TEACH Method is fairly intuitive and straightforward, the range of possibilities it provides can leave even the most experienced parent feeling a little uncertain.

If you're ready to put the TEACH Method to work for you, but you have a problem or special situation you're dealing with, this chapter is for you.

What Should I Do if the Consequences aren't Working?

One big advantage to the TEACH Method is that there is no limit to the number of logical consequences you can come up with. If one consequence isn't working, try another one! Find what works for you.

For example, if your child has a poor attitude, you could send him to his room until he's ready to speak appropriately, have him write a letter of apology or have him do extra work around the house, depending on what actually happened. You could even leave an event early and put him in charge of finding a way to make it up to your family. Get creative!

If one set of consequences isn't working and you need to adopt another, tell your children what you are doing and why. Explain to them that you are dedicated to making sure they grow up to be great people, and that you will continue to give more and more consequences until you find one that works.

Faced with the idea of more and more consequences, each one worse than the one before, hopefully your children will decide it's in their best interest to simply listen the first time, rather than risk incurring additional consequences they aren't going to like.

What About When the Children are Away from Home?

Just because your children are away from home for most or part of the day doesn't mean that you can't use the TEACH Method with them. You'll simply need to do most of the legwork before and after.

Set expectations and consequences before your children leave and follow through once they return home. Most adults will naturally give a warning and some type of consequence anyways if the children they are watching misbehave and you can give additional ones when they return home.

Your children may not experience the TEACH Method exactly as it is laid out in this book, but it should still be close enough to be effective.

What Should I Do if I am not my Children's Full-time Caregiver?

While the TEACH Method is obviously easier to implement if your are around your children day in and day out, you don't have to be your children's full-time caregiver to implement the method. In fact, you can still use the TEACH Method even if your children's full-time caregiver uses a different method.

You can still tell your children what you expect, set an example and have your children practice their best behavior before the babysitter arrives or you drop them off at daycare. You can hand out consequences and help your children process the situation once you reunite.

Sure, it would be better to hand out the consequences immediately, but as long as your children are old enough to remember what happened, it will still work just fine.

What Should I Do if Other Caregivers aren't on Board?

Co-parenting can be tricky—especially when you need to agree with someone who deserves equal say, such as the children's father. If the two of you don't agree, try to come to a compromise. Find out what he does or does not like about the TEACH Method and what questions or concerns he has. Perhaps you can tweak parts of it in a certain way that will leave you both happy or he can just do the consequences and let you take care of with the rest.

Perhaps you can convince him to give it a try for a few weeks, especially if what you are doing now isn't working, or you can convince him to let you try it while he continues with the method he likes. He may be more open to the idea once he sees how it works.

If it is a situation where you and your children's father are separated and each of you will be choosing your own disciplinary method, don't worry too much. Children are smart. They can learn multiple strategies.

Plus, the fact that you will tell your children exactly what you expect and what their consequences will be before you hand out the consequences will put them at a huge advantage when they're with you.

Just be consistent yourself and your children will adapt in time.Kids are pretty remarkable like that.

What Should I Do if it's not Working?

The TEACH Method is designed to make your life easier, not harder. If it isn't working for your family—don't use it! Find what works for you!

Do make sure that you are using the TEACH Method effectively before giving up, though, and be sure to give it time to work. If you've been overly permissive prior to trying this method, it may take a few weeks for your children to realize you are serious and to develop new habits and routines.

My hope for the TEACH Method is this: That you will have the knowledge you need to TEACH your children well, that your children will grow up to be wonderful, God-fearing people, and that you will have a happier, more fulfilling family experience because of it.

Whether your children are already pretty good listeners or you have a lot of work to do, I hope that by utilizing this Method, you'll all grow closer than ever before, and that you'll truly enjoy the years you have together.

After all, life is too short to waste them fighting with children over behavior. Let's TEACH and enjoy our children instead.

Good luck!

Additional Resources

Enjoyed this book and looking for more? Here are a few additional resources you might enjoy:

Putting God First: You put God first on Sunday mornings—what about the rest of the week? Practical and encouraging, "Putting God First" is a book that will help you do just that!

Prayer Cards: Prayer is powerful—are you putting it to good use? These cute prayer cards will help you cover your kids in the deep prayers they desperately need.

[Free] +Positive Parenting Challenge: Tired of the constant arguing? The +Positive Parenting Challenge is a free 6-day email challenge designed to help tired moms enjoy their kids once again.

Find all of these and more in the Equipping Godly Women shop!

http://equippinggodlywomen.com/shop

Made in the USA
Las Vegas, NV
27 September 2022

56025850R00059